Evangelism

139 Ideas and Quotes

Neil B. Wiseman, Editor

Beacon Hill Press of Kansas City
Kansas City, Missouri

Contents

Foreword

Billy Graham at the beginning of his ministry prayed, "O God, give me the whole world." This longing always characterizes serious Christians involved in reaching the lost for Christ. Evangelism is always motivated by such a soul burden.

Across the years the church has been blessed by Christians whose hearts were heavy with concern and whose eyes were wet with compassion. A personality trait, a serious nature, a spiritual gift—whatever the underlying forces, these daring giants brought sinners to Christ in an amazingly effective way.

In this book Dr. Neil B. Wiseman unearths gems, some that lay buried in older and out-of-print books, from the writings of these great souls. Here is a cache of 139 sparkling ideas covering a wide range of evangelism topics. Here laity and clergy alike can find the sparkle of inspiration and a lodestone for some burden, sermon preparation, and evangelism strategy.

Evangelism Ministries and the Nazarene Publishing House gladly present this work for the 1983 Conferences on Evangelism and also to commemorate our Diamond Anniversary as a denomination. It is circulated in anticipation that thousands of Nazarenes will be challenged to a renewed involvement in aggressive evangelism.

—BILL M. SULLIVAN, *Director*
Evangelism Ministries

Purpose

The historical record of evangelism in the Church of the Nazarene reads like a chapter from the Book of Acts. As in the days of the Early Church, the Nazarenes have had enormous victories and some disappointments. But always at the heart of the Nazarene movement there has been a committed evangelistic responsibility for the unbelieving neighbor next door, the perishing millions across the world, unreached folks in the next town, the rebellious backslider, and the wayward children of the church.

At significant transition points in the denomination's life, God has raised up leaders who preached and practiced this passion for souls. Both general and district superintendents, plus evangelists, pastors, and laity have joyously spent their energies and their resources in this great task. Across Nazarene history our evangelism vocabulary has expanded to include crusades, evangelistic home Bible classes, church planting, personal evangelism, and now church growth. But our purpose remains constant and powerful: the Church of the Nazarene exists for evangelism. The results—heaven has more citizens, genuine zest for life has been added to thousands of dreary lives, and the church has become larger and stronger through her evangelistic efforts.

In the fulfillment of our evangelism commitment, a literature of evangelism has been written by evangelizing folks and has been produced by the Nazarene Publishing House. Most entries in this book come from Nazarene literature. Some of this material is out of print, other sources have been reprinted, and recently new materials have been added. In a few instances the book draws from sources outside the denomination for helpful guidance.

This book is produced by Evangelism Ministries and the Division of Church Growth to provide ideas to stimulate evangelism in every church and to challenge every member of our global family to win souls. Nearly every idea in this volume has been discovered on the front lines of local church evangelism. No one person will cherish or agree with everything in this book, but there is something useful and inspiring for every disciple of Christ.

NEIL B. WISEMAN, *Editor*

1

Passion
for Evangelism

Why evangelize? The love of Christ constrains us to communicate the gospel to the whole world. The clear direction of the Savior to introduce everyone to His redemption challenges our commitments and resources. The abiding joy of leading another person to Christ makes us keep trying. The cleansing effect of true evangelism in a local church and in a denomination pushes us to do more. And our hearts are broken by the obvious end of the truly secular man living in a world that has gone mad. Without that driving force our church has no reason for existence.

Our forebears in this young denomination evangelized well. They knew their task, their world, and their God. Soul winning was the first priority. The results of their evangelization were well known to God and to us. Now our golden opportunity is here. We have had enough talk about evangelism. This is the time God has given us to plunge into the actual ministry of evangelization at every level of the church's life and activity. Now is the time to thrust in the harvest equipment to bring in the golden grain before it is forever too late. This is our day to evangelize.

Again we hear those haunting but motivating words of Jesus, "As my Father hath sent me, even so send I you" (John 20:21).

1. Theology and Evangelism

When evangelism is not fertilized, fed, and controlled by theology, it becomes a stylized performance seeking its effect through manipulative skills rather than the power of vision and the force of truth. Without each other both theology and evangelism are then, in one important sense, *unreal,* false to their own God-given nature; for all true theology has an evangelistic thrust, and all true evangelism is theology in action.

—James I. Packer

Our evangelists must be theologians and our theologians evangelists.

—James Denny

2. Evangelism, the Task of Every Believer

Since evangelism is everybody's business, its message is everybody's concern. There are five great truths which together form the biblical basis for the message of evangelism. They run like a golden thread through the Bible from Genesis 1 to Revelation 22. In summary statement they are:

Man apart from God's initiative is hopelessly involved in self-contradiction and lost.

God's remedy for the human plight is found in the death and resurrection of the Lord Jesus Christ.

Response in repentance and faith brings deliverance and new life to the individual.

Christian experience reaches its norm in entire sanctification with cleansing power for holy living in service to God and man.

The final triumph of God's purpose will be revealed in the coming of Christ to judge the quick and the dead.

—W. T. Purkiser

3. Evangelism, the Objective of All Church Organization

The object of every office, every department of the church, and of every organization in the church is the salvation of sinners, the sanctification of believers, the edification of the body of Christ. To this end let us work. To this end let us pray. To this end let us bend every effort and make every necessary sacrifice.

Holy evangelism must ever be our battle cry. The fiery passion of burning love for a perishing world must move us to great heroism and more daring undertakings for the salvation of all men.

—Board of General Superintendents
Sixth General Assembly (1923)

4. All Out for Souls

Go out to have revivals. Go out to win souls. Go out to preach holiness and get the people sanctified wholly. Go out to build the church. Go out to win and win gloriously. And may the God of Pentecost be your God. May the tongue of fire be given unto you. May the rich harvest field yield to your sharp sickles, and may you bring many sheaves at last to the Master's feet.

—R. V. DeLong

5. Burden for Revival

The soul who has experienced [a burden for revival] will not need dictionaries and commentaries to explain what it means ... Every prophet of God, from Noah's day to the present, who has counted for aught in the salvation of men, has been acquainted, to a greater or lesser degree, with the heart-pressure and sense of soul agony that possess the one who is burdened for the church or world.

—*Beulah Christian,* 1902

6. Personal Need for Revival

When asked how to start a revival, Gypsy Smith replied: "Go home, lock yourself in your room, kneel down in the middle of the floor, draw a chalk mark all around yourself, and ask God to start the revival inside that chalk mark. When He has answered your prayer the revival will be on."

—Quoted by Fletcher C. Spruce

7. Personal Concern—Basis for Evangelism

It may be easy for us to converse with people. We may even have an excellent gospel proclamation and plan, but if we do not love them and accept them as they are, our evangelism has no integrity. People don't care how much we know until they know how much we care.

—Don Gibson

8. Evangelism—A Labor of Love

Evangelism is the labor of love. It is such a work as can be inspired only by the "love which is shed abroad in the heart by the Holy Ghost" (Rom. 5:5). No other motive will be sufficient to drive the church to her great task of world evangelism. Furthermore, if the church does carry on the program in a merely formal fashion, it will be without effect. The unbelieving world can be persuaded only by those whose hearts are hot with holy passion and whose lives give evidence of having been empowered by the indwelling of the Holy Spirit. The great cause of the present plight of Christendom is that the love which inspires labor for the lost is lacking.

—G. B. Williamson

9. Lostness of the Sinner

A sinner is dead in trespasses and sins, so Paul writes in Eph. 2:1. He may be a nice person who does the "right things," belongs to the "right group," and possesses financial security, but he is spiritually dead unless he has accepted Christ as his personal Saviour. If he dies without repenting and accepting Jesus Christ as his Saviour, he will spend eternity in hell. Jesus said: "Except ye repent, ye shall all likewise perish" (Luke 13:3, 5).

Jesus concludes His discussion of the need for faithfulness in ministering in His name to the needs of others with these words: "Inasmuch as ye did it not to one of the least of these, ye did it not to me. And these shall go away into everlasting punishment: but the righteous into life eternal" (Matt. 25:45-46).

—Bennett Dudney

10. Need for Passion

There is not enough heartbreak over the lost, not enough soul burden, not enough groaning and weeping and fasting and crying.

—J. B. Chapman

11. Love Is Evangelism's Foundation

Love avoids the impersonal approach and does not require a religious vocabulary (even though it be fortified with scripture). There is no substitute for a quiet, friendly, personal talk, away from the eyes and ears of others.

Love is never intent on making a witness merely to relieve conscience. Out of real concern for another, love takes time to listen. Love does not run away!

Love quickly sees the heart-needs of others. Love remains at leisure from itself—sensitive and responsive to others. Love lets *God's love* come through, at any time, any place, with any person, age, or race.

Love is never in a hurry. Love never pushes. Love keeps a quiet heart, ready for the Spirit's guidance. Love is patient and waits for God's timing.

When love witnesses, it does not seek to make people over, nor to dictate behavior. With quiet confidence, love speaks of her Beloved (Christ) and of security and trust in Him.

Love does not substitute methods for a living relationship. Love is sensitive and seeks to discern where the Spirit is already at work in another. Love does not go off on a tangent of its own.

—Rosalind Rinker

12. Revivals Brought Nazarenes into Existence

We were born in a revival atmosphere and we must continue to live in such an atmosphere if we hope to live at all. It is a genuine holiness evangelism that brought the church into existence and the same type of evangelism is essential to our existence and success. Let there be no tendency to substitute programs and sentimentalism for old-fashioned, Holy Ghost, God-sent revivals.

—R. T. Williams

13. Revivals of History

There were at least two historic outstanding facts about great revivals. First, they presented great central, redemptive truths and availed themselves of inexhaustible resources which God wants to give His followers. In divine strength and power they offered salvation to multitudes and brought new hope to the world. During these periods the Church became mighty as a world force.

Second, these revivals came at a time when people were

anxious to turn to God. They were oppressed by tyranny. Their physical circumstances were almost unbearable. Sin and wickedness in high places with tragic governmental, social, and religious consequences had caused them to long for relief and salvation that only God could give.

—V. H. Lewis

14. History of Nazarene Evangelists

The measure of emphasis on evangelism can be judged by the fact that the First General Assembly *Journal* (1907) printed a list of authorized evangelists. Even though there were only 100 churches in the whole denomination, there were 67 on the roll of authorized evangelists. This amazing army of evangelistic warriors had to hold meetings under brush arbors, in schools, on courthouse lawns, and anywhere that people could be found, if they were to keep busy. The small number of churches could not possibly use more than 15 full-time evangelists. This meant that most of the evangelists had to launch out on their own and hold hundreds of revivals in places where there were no churches. The heroic sacrifices represented by this type of dedicated service reflect the driving enthusiasm to kindle the fires of revival everywhere.

—Mendell Taylor

15. Christ Is the Gospel

It is not so much that Jesus came to teach a gospel as that He came to be the gospel. In Him, God not only tells us what the Father is and what He would have us to be; He shows us.

Christ said—not, "I describe the way, and tell you the truth, and inform you about the life"—but, "I *am* the way, the truth, and the life."

—W. T. Purkiser

16. Evangelism Is More than Activity

Just as inactivity is no sure sign of unbelief or falling away, so busyness in the "work of the church" is no proof of faith or an understanding of grace. Many a church member has fallen victim to the danger described in *Murder in a Cathedral* by T. S. Eliot:

> The last temptation is the greatest treason:
> To do the right thing for the wrong reason.

When a dizzying round of churchly—or "churchy"—activities allows a person to neglect home and family or to soothe a guilty conscience or to earn "points" with God, that person needs the liberating, forgiving word of the gospel as much as anyone. There should be no condescension here: the "super-active" member needs it for the same reason as I do. I, too, become self-seeking and self-justifying in my service and need to be "freed up" to love and serve effectively.

—Ralph W. Quere

17. Need for Revivals

Can we fulfill our mission as a holiness church committed to holiness evangelism without revivals?—the answer is an emphatic "NO!"

To be a redemptive agency in this sin-scarred world—we must have revivals.

To resist the incredible pressures of a church in transition—we must have revivals.

To maintain our loyalties to our doctrines and our standards—we must have revivals.

To fulfill the dreams and realize the vision of our founders—we must have revivals.

To fulfill our destiny and to realize our full potential as a God-called, God-directed, God-empowered, distinctively holiness church—we must have revivals.

To hand on a spiritually vigorous and dynamic church to our children—we must have revivals.

To have an evangelism that is more than a mockery of our mission, but that is a genuine holiness evangelism that sees souls saved and believers sanctified wholly and that is at once the dynamic of the church and the only adequate answer to a confused and chaotic world, then we must—we simply must—have revivals!

—C. William Fisher

18. Revival Prescription

First, let a few Christians get thoroughly right with God and themselves. This is the prime essential! If this is not done, the rest I say will come to nothing. Second, let them bind themselves together to pray for revival until God opens the heavens and comes down. Third, let them put themselves at the disposal of God, for Him to use as He sees fit in winning others to Christ. That is all! I have given this prescription around the world. It has been taken by many churches and communities and it never has failed to bring revival!

—R. A. Torrey

19. Revivals Can Be Expected . . .

• When the providence of God indicates that a revival is at hand

• When the wickedness of the wicked grieves and humbles and distresses Christians

• When Christians have a spirit of prayer for a revival

• When the attention of ministers is especially directed to this particular object

• When Christians begin to confess their sins to one another

• When Christians are found willing to make the sacrifices necessary to carry it on

• When ministers and professors are willing to have God promoted by what instruments He pleases

—Mendell Taylor

20. Asbury College Revival

The spontaneous movement of the Holy Spirit was awesome to behold. Confessions mingled with shouts of praise; old enmities melted in divine sweetness; restitutions were made. There was release—freedom—embracing—joy unspeakable. Love was real. A thousand hearts joined in adoration to a mighty God.

For eight days and nights it lasted. Classes were forgotten. Academic work came to a standstill. The reality of another world took precedence over every other concern. As people experienced God's cleansing and infilling, they went out to tell others of the wonderful works of God. The flame of revival spread to other schools and churches across the land and around the world. Who can reckon its ultimate influence?

Those of us who have seen this happen have learned anew that God's power shines only through broken and contrite spirits. Self-disclosure in one person encourages honesty in another troubled heart. And by sharing our weaknesses we are drawn closer to each other for strength. That is why it can be said that revival begins when we quit confessing other people's sins and start confessing our own.

—Robert E. Coleman

21. Revivals Needed to Revive Church

A church or a person does not have to be backslidden to need revival. Shortly after the mighty Pentecost, the early Christians needed a fresh infilling of the Spirit because of threats and because of the task confronting them (Acts 4:23-31). A person can feel himself spiritually depleted in the Lord's work.

A church can feel itself weak after addressing itself to exhausting ministries and programs in carrying out the Lord's work. At such times the heart cries for renewal and revival.

Lived there a person who did not come to a place in his Christian life that seemed to him to be a dry place? And do not churches come to the same place? There may be many reasons, but to each of us come those times when it seems it has been altogether too long since there has been an outpouring of the Holy Spirit into our lives and churches. We have come to a dry place. At such times, the Lord has for us the refreshing showers of revival.

—Ponder Gilliland

22. Total Commitment Needed for Evangelism

Dawson Trotman put it bluntly when he said: "God can do more through one man who is 100% dedicated to Him than through 100 men 90% dedicated to Him." Half-hearted, weak-kneed, compromising obedience will never challenge a sleeping church to rise up and rescue perishing souls from the jaws of hell. Our highly sophisticated society in the Church may look upon such unfettered zeal for Christ as fanaticism, but it is still the way the Holy Spirit works in revival.

—Robert E. Coleman

23. Evangelism Defined

Evangelism is simply telling all people everywhere the good news of salvation through Christ in such a way as to lead as many as possible to saving faith, entire sanctification, and practical commitment to the work of the Kingdom in the fellowship of the Church.

—W. T. Purkiser

24. Love Is the Motive for Evangelism

The love of Christ filling our hearts moves us to care for those whom God loves and for whom He gave His Son. Out of this holy compassion the dynamic for a compelling evangelism and social concern is born. Duty becomes a joy. In revival we want to help the oppressed and afflicted. Love naturally overflows when hearts are full.

—Robert E. Coleman

25. Revival Involvement

Every believer associated with your church shares responsibility for the evangelistic revival meeting. Great revivals depend on wholehearted participation by the entire congregation. Every member and friend of the church should be made to feel needed in the revival effort.

Through your efforts, every Christian should come to believe that he is personally responsible for faith, attendance, prayer, and giving for revival. Participation is greater when everyone understands his individual responsibility and knows he is part of an organized group working toward a common revival goal. An opportunity to serve should be provided for everyone.

—Stephen Manley

26. Revival Potential

Have you ever thought seriously about what a great spiritual revival could do for your church and community?

—What would happen if all the church family were to be personally involved in prayer for the lost?

—What would happen in your church if it became the center of community attention because of the life-changing events at your revival meeting?

—What would happen in your church if scores of your church family were trained in personal evangelism, altar work, follow-through, and Bible study?

—What would happen in your church if everyone who responded to an altar call were to be incorporated immediately into a warm and responsive relationship with a Christian friend?

—Michael Ross

27. Evangelism Advances the Church

Evangelism is our method of advance as a church. We offer neither ritual nor ceremony as a substitute for salvation. Souls can know Christ as a personal Saviour in a personal experience. The only way we know to bring this to pass is through evangelism. We must not and shall not fail to evangelize! Our church was brought into being through the fires of evangelism. May its flame ever burn high on the altars of our churches.

—V. H. Lewis

28. Evangelism Opportunities

God is at work in remarkable ways today. The shock waves of an "evangelism explosion" continue to spread across the land. Never have so many people been open to the gospel in so many places. In these challenging days, the church must be alert to the fact that evangelism is not an option . . . it is an imperative.

If businesses have sales meetings, stores have bargain days, and civic clubs have motivational conventions, then certainly the church must continue to promote revival campaigns. Someone has said, "Without revivals, the church becomes a social club existing to pamper its parishioners."

—John J. Hancock

29. Biblical Doctrine of Evangelism

A Bible-based doctrine of evangelism embraces the following:

- Those who are unsaved are lost. Not going to be lost,

23

but lost now. No matter how likable they are, how brilliant they may be, or what good neighbors they make, without Christ they are lost.

• Hell and heaven are real. Jesus thought hell was real. He was so convinced of it that He left heaven to die on the Cross to save us from it. We must warn a world that has blotted all the passages of divine judgment out of the Bible.

• The redeeming love and acts of Jesus Christ are the answer to man's predicament—the only answer. We must maintain a firm faith in the power of the atoning Christ. He is bigger than any sin, greater than any situation. His blood can cleanse the deepest stain.

• Holiness is God's standard for His people. Full salvation, freedom from sin, is God's plan for every believer. Purity and the indwelling Holy Spirit can be ours. Is not this the greatest gift that God gives us on earth—the life of God in the soul of man?

• The Great Commission is a personal command to every Christian. Jesus has placed the responsibility for winning the lost squarely on our shoulders.

—Wesley Tracy

30. Holiness and Revivals

The experience of holiness in the individual heart and the work of revival in the church, are closely associated. God has joined them together, and no man should attempt to put them asunder.

—W. A. Powers

For what has the Lord called the Church of the Nazarene into existence: To preach holiness? Yes. But for more than that; to evangelize, to have revivals, to save sinners, as well as lead believers into sanctification, to preach the gospel of the Son of God, to stir men to seek the face of God.

When we cease to be evangelistic, we cease to carry out our divine commission, and that moment we begin to decay. Every pastor, every evangelist, every missionary, every worker must be a soul winner. . . . The dominant note of our movement should and must be Evangelism.

—R. T. Williams

31. Purity and Power as Evangelism Sources

Purity is a constant, but power is a variable. There are no gradations in purity, no ups and downs—your heart is either pure or it isn't pure; your heart is either clean or it isn't clean. God's word is, "If we walk in the light, as he is in the light, we have fellowship one with another, and the blood of Jesus Christ his Son cleanseth us from all sin" (1 John 1:7).

Power, however, is a variable. Power ebbs and flows. The line on the graph of our power is a fluctuating line; it rises and falls. It is the plus of the life of holiness. There will never be a time in a truly sanctified life when the line of power will dip below the line of purity. In other words, there will never be a time when that life will be totally without spiritual power. But the danger is that we will allow the line of power to get so close to the line of purity that the only testimony of our lives will be that we are nice, that we are decent, that we are respectable, that we are religious. But one can be all of those without any power at all from God.

—C. William Fisher

32. The Message of Evangelism

As he lay in a Roman dungeon awaiting his martyrdom, Paul passed to Timothy the torch that is still aflame: "The things that thou hast heard of me among many witnesses, the same commit thou to faithful men, who shall be able to teach others also" (2 Tim. 2:2).

What things?

The things and only the things that were in perfect accord with what was divinely written in various countries over a period of about fifteen centuries by forty or more men of God who separately and solitarily were "moved by the Holy Ghost." The amazing unity of the Word of God as revealed through Chaldea-trained Abraham, Egypt-trained Moses, Judah-trained David, Babylon-trained Daniel, Persia-trained Nehemiah was not disturbed a feather's weight nor deflected a hair's breadth by Roman-trained Paul. The things were precisely what the others taught, so far as they taught them for the single and sufficient reason that all were taught of God.

"The same commit thou."

"The same"; nothing more; nothing less; nothing other. The same in substance; the same in emphasis; the same in presentation; the same in power.

—J. N. Barnette

33. Jesus' Method of Evangelism Training

His method of training [the disciples] this vanguard of His church is simply to draw them together around Himself. He does not establish a formal school nor does He prescribe a creed which His disciples must profess. All He asks is for them to follow Him. His teaching is incarnated in His own Person. By following Him they know the truth, the way, and the life. In His company the disciples learn what it means to live in God, and also how to communicate His life to man.

—Robert E. Coleman

34. Front Line of Evangelism

The front line is always right next to you. The man who works next to you; the woman who sits at the next desk; the one who is sitting by you on the bus, train, or plane; the family living in the next apartment or next door—are the front line for you. Right here is where we so often fail. We have eyes on the needs far away. But the harvest field for you, for me, is right next to each of us.

—V. H. Lewis

35. Revivals Possible Everywhere

There is no pastor He cannot renew and no church He cannot revive. Since He is the risen Lord there is no place His Spirit cannot go and no situation His voice cannot penetrate. There is no cave He cannot visit and no island He cannot reach. The spirit of revival can come anywhere God can go, and God's Spirit can go anywhere one or more persons are gathered in His name. Christ specializes in bringing revival to small, hard places where people have every reason to be discouraged.

—Leslie Parrott

2

Revivals and Public Evangelism

Ask Nazarenes how they were converted and they are likely to tell you that they found Christ at a Nazarene altar, probably either in a revival meeting, in a camp meeting, or in an evangelistic service in the normal schedule of their church. Revivals and public evangelism have been at the heart of the Church of the Nazarene from the beginning. Many of our churches were born in home mission revivals. Our colleges affectionately build revivals into their calendars and curricula. Nearly every Nazarene minister has preached in a revival meeting somewhere. Nazarene evangelists are busy drawing the gospel net, and Nazarene pastors are preaching for a decision. Public evangelism is one of our specialties. Nazarenes believe in and practice public evangelism. A number of helpful ideas for public evangelism follow.

36. The Power of Evangelistic Preaching

It is impossible to understand how any man can be a Bible preacher without being evangelistic in his spirit and in his message. If he lives with the prophets and expounds their message he is truly evangelistic. If he sits at Jesus' feet and learns of Him, he will be endued with evangelistic power. If he takes the apostles as his pattern, he will be just as evangelistic as he is apostolic. This truth the whole church needs to understand. The Bible preacher is the one and the only one who is truly evangelistic.

—G. B. Williamson

37. Relationship of Public and Personal Evangelism

Is the day of mass evangelism coming to a close? No! Church history tells us that the great revivals in the past have always used mass evangelism. We need that kind of revival today. Mass evangelism combined with personal witnessing can make the church more effective than ever before.

—V. H. Lewis

Each evangelistic method fits neatly into the whole of New Testament evangelism. Methods do not *compete* with each other; they *complete* each other. The evangelistic preaching service is an example of this. The church members and the preacher are partners in evangelism. Unless the members are faithful in personal evangelism and visitation, there will likely be no unsaved persons present to hear the sermon.

—Wesley Tracy

38. Need for Christ-Centered Preaching

Our regular Sunday-by-Sunday pulpit diet must be Christ-centered. Much of our preaching is no longer personal but only institutional. We have forgotten the worth of the soul and the dignity of man and the individual responsibility for sin. We have placed our emphasis on budgets and machinery and program and methods. This diet will never pave the way for a revival. Instead of having a church-centered pulpit we must have a Christ-centered pulpit. It goes without saying that a preacher who is worth his salt will be loyal to every phase of his district, general, and local program. But it also goes without saying that a preacher whose message lifts up the Master will pave the way for revival survival.

—Fletcher C. Spruce

39. Preaching Is Basic Evangelistic Method

Preaching as the primary public proclamation of the Word utilizes evangelistic crusades, mass media, and especially worship services for the work of evangelism. Despite criticism and loss of confidence in some quarters regarding the spoken word, preaching remains the basic form of communicating the Good News. A sermon takes a Word of God addressed to people in a different time and place and redirects the message to men in our day. The situation to which the biblical text is addressed—insofar as that can be discerned—must be taken seriously and then transcended as the gospel is applied to the ills, needs, problems, and questions of people today.

—Ralph W. Quere

40. Preaching as God's Method

Although pulpit evangelism has suffered at the hands of its critics in recent years, a method which, from the day of Pentecost, has been of incalculable effect in spreading Christianity throughout the earth is not likely to become outmoded in our generation.

—Roy C. Angell

41. Evangelistic Pastoral Preaching

The first and last requirement for a successful pastor is that he shall have a high conception of his calling and a deep and passionate concern for the salvation of men. He must exemplify the spirit of evangelism always. The pastor is to be a "hound of heaven," always in hot pursuit of men who need the Saviour. Such a spirit, deep in his inmost being, will produce an effective overtone in his appeal whether it be in public or in private.

—G. B. Williamson

42. Simple Preaching Needed for Evangelism

As to the content, a preacher in his study may think in technicolor, but his content for an evangelistic sermon must be as plain as black and white, and as clear and as direct and as simple as he can make it. It is easy to "muddy up the water" or be mystifying. It takes hard work to express profound mysteries and realities and concepts like love and sin and Deity and redemption and judgment in simple words that really communicate with the listeners. And what difference does it make how profound, or clever, or scholarly the sermon if the people don't know what the preacher is talking about, or worse, are not stirred enough to care?

—C. William Fisher

43. Public Invitation

If a man expects to see results at an altar of prayer, he must be gifted not only in preaching, but also in exhortation. He must know how to draw his net, to win decisions, to move men to action.

—G. B. Williamson

44. Objectives for Public Evangelism

In planning for public evangelism, I set up these basic objectives:

• *Unification.* I want to bring my people together in spiritual atmosphere for a set period of time. This allows them to play, pray, work, worship, and fellowship together. In the climate of revival, they can get to know each other better, find themselves in "one accord," and discover the reality expressed in the chorus "We Are One in the Bond of Love."

• *Inspiration and motivation.* I want my co-worker, the evangelist—my revivalist—to proclaim spiritual truth in ways that will edify the saints, encourage new Christians, clarify Bible concepts, and challenge my people to holy living.

• *Evangelization and salvation.* I want the way of redemption clearly and warmheartedly presented to the sinner, the way of holiness proclaimed to the believer, and the way back to God's love revealed to the backslider. I want the "edge of the crowd" Christian encouraged to move into the heart of the fellowship.

• *Intensification and perpetuation of the church's total ministry.* I want my church to "come alive" under the leadership of the Holy Spirit. My objective is to experience renewal that will lift the "love life" of my people and set their direction for more effective and dynamic ministries and outreach.

—John J. Hancock

45. Objectives of Public Evangelism

• *Mission:*
  Revivals, evangelism, church growth
• *Motive:*
  Love for Jesus
• *Method:*
  Constant prayer, complete commitment, constant involvement, continual obedience.

—Stephen Manley

46. Total Force of Church Growth

Mass evangelism demands and must command the total force of the local church. It can be a great outreach and a bounteous harvest time for the work of personal evangelism, or it can be just another effort that causes laymen to wonder if it pays. Let us never be content with an effort that fails to reach out to the lost and unchurched. We must make our churches powerful in spirit, organization, operation, pulpit, and pew by means of evangelism.

—V. H. Lewis

47. Special Groups to Increase Revival Attendance

Pew-filling enthusiasm results by scheduling the evangelist for special ministries. Following a service, a specified group could meet with the evangelist for a brief time of fellowship and sharing.

● *Fellowship Ministry*
This would be an all-church fellowship following the first service. Refreshments and informal discussion could be followed by a personal word from the evangelist.

● *Leadership Ministry*
Lay leaders would be invited to fellowship with the evangelist following a service. He could be an encouragement to key leaders.

● *Men's Ministries*
How about a Saturday morning prayer breakfast or a special get-together before or after a service? In some churches a men's choir would be a possibility, or provision could be made for men's testimonies on a certain night.

● *Ladies' Ministries*
A luncheon for all the women in the congregation allows the evangelist and/or his wife to speak specifically to women's interests. Special women's prayer meetings are another possibility. The idea is to get all the women together to affirm their value to the church and to address their particular needs.

● *Teen Ministries*
An afterglow with the evangelist is a good idea. If teens are to be truly touched by the revival, their personal exposure to the evangelist must be increased.

● *Children's Ministries*
Children are people, too. They need to know how important they are to the church. You might want to plan some event

especially for them and expose them to the personal ministry of the evangelist.

—Manley and Ross

48. Sunday School Classes Increase Revival Attendance

The evangelist suggested this plan. Each class would attend at least two nights during the revival—as a group. The teacher would designate which two nights were most suitable for his class. Each night the class with the highest percentage of enrollment present would receive a special mention. This would give the pupils incentive to work. Members of their families not enrolled in other classes would count for the class. In the nursery and kindergarten classes emphasis would be upon getting parents to attend.

—Mary E. Latham

49. Hindrances to Revivals

• The revival will cease when Christians become mechanical in their attempt to promote revival. When their faith is strong and their hearts are warm and mellow and their prayers full of holy emotion and their words with power, then the work goes on.

• A revival will cease when Christians get the idea that the work will go on without their aid.

• A revival will cease when the church prefers to attend to their own concerns rather than God's business. They begin to think they cannot afford sufficient time from their worldly employment to carry on a revival.

• A revival will cease when Christians refuse to render

to the Lord according to the benefits received. God has opened the windows of heaven to a church and poured them out a blessing, and then He reasonably expects them to bring the tithes into the storehouse.

—Mendell Taylor

50. A Variety of Evangelists Needed

It is not fair to a congregation to use just one type of preacher—for instance, one who appeals only to the intellect; or one who simply teaches the Bible in a seminary-type ministry; or one who thunders continuously a message of judgment. All of these approaches are needed and should be seen as the various hues of the evangelistic rainbow. Churches can easily become unbalanced when their people are continuously fed on one kind of diet.

—Charles Millhuff

In choosing evangelists a church should not choose all of the same type. It is very wholesome for a church to have some revivals in which the evangelist is of the teaching type, one who unfolds the deep things of God and leads the people of the church into more glorious experiences of grace. At other times the church needs the man who is gifted in the denouncing of sin, in the calling of men to repentance by proclaiming the judgments of God, and in warning men of the rewards and punishments of eternity.

—G. B. Williamson

51. The Message and the Messenger

A preacher, after all, is just a messenger. His primary purpose is to deliver a "message." A Western Union messenger knocks at a door and hands a telegram to the occupant. The person may rip open the envelope and then burst into sobbing because it contains news of some tragedy to a loved one or friend. Or the recipient may smile because the message gives some wonderful news. It isn't the messenger; it is the message that makes the difference. And so it is in the case of a preacher, especially an evangelistic preacher: he is a messenger, and it isn't the messenger that matters, it is the message. It is the message of God's love, the message of what happens when we accept that love, the message of the consequences of rejecting that love. And no gospel is complete that does not include both the promise and the warning.

—C. William Fisher

52. Pastoral Prayer and Evangelism

Seldom does a pastor lead his people in prayer on a Sunday morning without there being some persons present who need divine forgiveness. Should not this high and holy moment of worship include those persons whose hearts may be crying out for pardon, even when they are reluctant to admit it? Sometimes the evangelistic appeal of the Holy Spirit is very tender and soft and quiet. Jesus was aware of this. When He taught His own followers how to pray . . . and the prayer was ever so short . . . He did not overlook the prayer for forgiveness.

The list could be extended to cover all the activities of the church. This is not to say that all of them are basically evangelistic. It is to suggest . . . perhaps to insist . . . that if the

Holy Spirit could not make an evangelistic thrust in every existing activity or ministry of the church, that activity probably has no part in the program of the church.

—Ponder W. Gilliland

53. Evangelists' Pay

If a church is to err at all, it had better be on the side of generosity with an evangelist. Pastors and church boards have sometimes driven an evangelist to desperation because they have not given him a living compensation. If a figure is to be set by the church board, the evangelist has a right to know what it is to be. If it is based on the pay of the pastor of the church, then it should be remembered that the evangelist supports his family at home, provides his own house, pays his own traveling expenses, and has many other obligations that do not devolve upon a pastor. It is deplorable to see an evangelist grasping for money; it is no less deplorable to see a church board parsimonious and niggardly in the compensation of an evangelist.

—G. B. Williamson

54. Evangelistic Music

John Wesley repeatedly warned his churches and societies that if they lost the spontaneity out of their singing they would lose something vital and attractive out of their movement. That is true of any movement that believes in and emphasizes heart experience. Let us never sacrifice that spontaneity and reality in our singing, even under the guise of "musicianship."

That is not to say, of course, that the singing and music in an evangelistic service are mainly for the heel and not for the head. Experience songs can be sung well, and in a spirit of reverence.

—C. William Fisher

A performance in vocal gymnastics grieves the Spirit and often disgusts thoughtful people. For revival work the great gospel songs that give expression to the experience that God has wrought in the hearts of His believing children are the most desirable. Gospel songs should not be set to ragtime music or perverted until they sound like modern jazz. They need only to be sung with the Spirit and with the understanding.

—G. B. Williamson

55. Invitation Advice

Do not be defeated. Do not let the devil bluff you out of an invitation. He will try it. He will make all kinds of suggestions, such as, "There is no conviction, the hour is late, you will drive folks away." Or he will pick out some individual in the audience and suggest because of him you should not give an invitation. Do not be defeated. We should always remember that the devil is a liar and the father of lies.

—Jarrette Aycock

56. Invitations Are Expected

Christians hope for an invitation and 90 percent of the

sinners expect it. Twice in my ministry I have received a note from the unsaved rebuking me because I did not give them an opportunity to come to the altar.

We are not suggesting that an invitation should always be given or that it should always be lengthy. Yet we are saying that we should try to get the mind of God as to how and when the invitation should be given and not be defeated by a suggestion of the devil.

—Jarrette Aycock

57. Invitation Victory and Prayer

Many spiritually minded people have learned, during the service and especially during the invitation, to make the persons on their left and on their right a prayer group of two or three. When such people are agreed in faith concerning the service and in behalf of the unsaved, it is amazing how God can work.

—Orville W. Jenkins

Do not let the fact that there seems to be a lethargy or deadness in the service defeat or deceive you. I have yielded to this feeling and closed the service and had good Christians come around and say, "God was here tonight, and lots of conviction on the people." It was I who was dead, tired, and afflicted with lethargy. I was deceived, whipped out, and defeated in what might have been a fruitful service.

If we could only remember that Jesus said, "I am with you alway"; you may be tired, but "I will help thee."

—Jarrette Aycock

58. Variety of Public Evangelism

In Long Beach, Calif., First Church, we did more than merely schedule two meetings a year for evangelistic emphasis. During my eight years there we had revival or evangelistic meetings.

We also had
- Deeper Life Campaigns
- Wesleyan Festivals of Faith
- Youth Revivals
- Other one- to three-day special emphases

All of these were in addition to a consistent ministry of
- Regular pastoral evangelism preaching
- Evangelism in Sunday School classes
- Evangelistic emphases in youth groups
- Day camps for children
- Summer offensives for youth
- Personal evangelism

—Ponder W. Gilliland

59. Things to Avoid in Invitations

- Avoid anything that detracts from the effectiveness of your message, especially near the close. Anything that detracts from the sinfulness of sin, the love of Christ, and the necessity of salvation should never be admitted into the services.

- Avoid using illustrations which are illogical, unreasonable, extreme, or ridiculous. In our age of travel and modern education, superstition is almost a thing of the past and anything bordering on it will prove more ridiculous than effective.

- Avoid making the price of salvation so high that people

will feel they cannot afford it. Many things are easier explained and settled after they come to the altar.

• Avoid making your proposition so weak and easy that to respond becomes meaningless. The Scriptures say, He "commandeth all men every where to repent."

• Avoid making rash statements, such as, "The Holy Ghost left that man tonight." It might keep him from ever trying to find God; and then he might get saved in the next service, which would place you in a poor light as a prophet.

• Avoid speaking disparagingly of any other church. There may be people in the audience who have strong ties of kinship or sentiment with that church, and unkind remarks, even when true, may drive them away. Crowds are too small these days; we cannot afford to lose anyone from our audiences.

• Avoid public issues from the pulpit. You may be right, but someone is sure to take the other fellow's side.

• Avoid making a hobby of nonessentials and preaching your convictions as though they were essential to salvation. The exhortation of the Scriptures is "Preach the Word."

• Avoid using illustrations that are extreme and treating them as though such instances are common. I dare say all the vivid ones you know are the exception rather than the rule.

—Jarrette Aycock

60. Sanctification—A Goal of Evangelism

Preaching the new birth is never more than the bare threshold of authentic, fulfilling evangelism. Being converted was the beginning, not the end. Conversion was the rainbow which arched the entrance onto the pathway of a lifelong pilgrimage in Christ. Wesley warned his followers against the saving of souls they did not have time to nurture. He not only taught his laymen to win souls, but also to help stabilize young converts by enrolling them in a small group of helpful Christians.

The sanctified life is the goal and end of all valid evangelistic endeavor, and this implies a lifelong process. If Wesley were alive today, he would not be very excited about hit-and-run personal evangelism unless there were the follow-through to nurture. New converts need the life sustaining fellowship of a loving congregation where there is instruction, inspiration, and support. Wesley was 200 years ahead of himself with his own small-group movement.

—Leslie Parrott

61. Definite Invitations and Fourth Propositions

God has helped me to help thousands on what I call "The Fourth Proposition." This was suggested to me by hearing Dr. Chapman say, "We invite people forward to be saved, reclaimed, and filled with the Spirit; and I sometimes wonder if we should not have a fourth proposition inviting Christians to the altar to get help."

Here are about the words I use in giving this invitation. "I have been inviting you each night to come forward and seek on three counts, to be saved, to be reclaimed, or to be filled with the Spirit. The altar is still open for anyone in need of any of these three. But tonight I wish to emphasize to you a fourth proposition, not to the unsaved or backslider, but to the Christian.

"This is not for reconsecration, or 'get closer to God' appeal, which is so often given, but a definite proposition as to your own personal needs.

"How many Christians are there here who say: 'Preacher, I am not backslidden. I love God and I am trying to hold on to Him, but I will admit I have lost ground. I have seen better days spiritually. I am not at the place I used to be.

"'I have not gone back to the old habits, the old haunts, or the old sins, but I have been so busy trying to make a living, send my children to school, and support my family that I find my soul lean. I have been so busy in legitimate things that I have neglected weightier matters.'

"You definitely admit you are not where you once were, and where you ought to be and want to be. Would you be willing to come and kneel and let us gather around and pray for you?"

I have seen many helped in this way.

—Jarrette Aycock

62. Objective of Altar Service

The objective of the evangelistic service is not merely to get people to the altar, but to get them right with God. When people come to the altar the battle isn't won; in a very real sense it is just beginning. The devil doesn't care how close to victory a person comes, just so long as he doesn't say that final and crucial "yes" to God.

—C. William Fisher

63. Advice to Altar Workers

• Find out what the individual is seeking: to be saved, reclaimed, sanctified—or has he come because he is over-conscientious and the enemy is trying to make him doubt?

• Refrain from making any statement in your exhortation or prayer that would lead the individual to think the altar, praying out loud, looking up, raising his hands, or any attitude of the body is essential to finding God.

• Drive home through exhortation and scripture the truth that God is ready, anxious, and willing to meet the seeker's need the moment he meets the conditions laid down in God's Word. Impress upon him that it is the attitude of the heart, and not any outward act or physical position, that is essential.

• Study the seeker with whom you deal. It is a well-known fact that there are some who, if you can get them to pray aloud, lift up their hands, or look up, will be broken up and thus find it easier to pray and believe God. It is also known that there are others so constituted that if you urge any of these things upon them too strongly they will be driven away. The efficient worker will study the temperament of each individual and will deal with him accordingly.

• Do not ask anyone if he is willing to preach or go to the mission field. Ofttimes the enemy takes advantage of this and uses it to keep a seeker from getting through to God, or causes him to think he is called when he is not. Either is disastrous. Let God raise these questions.

—Jarrette Aycock

64. Altar Service Prayer

The seeker didn't come to the altar to talk to people, but to talk to God. And many well-meaning people have diluted or destroyed this crucial sense of crisis by talking to a seeker too soon.

The crisis needs to develop and intensify until the heart is willing to meet whatever demand of repentance or surrender God is requiring. God forgive us for rushing in with talk and admonition, no matter how well-meaning, and destroying this sense of crisis. The seeker may get up with his head full of his sins, and empty of God's grace. This is not a spiritual victory.

That is not to say, of course, that a person who is new to what is involved in crisis experience should not have instruction. But the instruction should not be so theologically involved that it will intrude into the developing sense of sin and crisis too soon, or the conviction for sin will evaporate into mere talk.

It seems to be so much easier to "talk" or to "sing" in the altar service than it is to pray. But the praying is the important and vital part. A seeker can get through without the talking and the singing, but he can't get through without praying.

—C. William Fisher

65. Altar Call for New Christians

After the altar has been opened to sinners, the unsanctified, and the backslidden, the pastor of a soul-winning church will want then to invite those who have accepted Christ during the week to come forward to confirm their decision publicly.

It would be well for a person who has led someone to the Lord that week and has brought him to the service to alert the pastor. Thus the pastor can be sure to include in his invitation the call for new converts.

There are many bonuses in making the call for new Christians a regular part of the invitation:

—It highlights the important work of personal evangelism.

—It shows that the pastor and the church *expect* Christians to be soul winners.

—It honors those who have indeed been active in the greatest Christian task—winning people to Christ.

—It goes a long way toward tying new believers to the church.

—Wesley Tracy

66. Testimonies Following Altar Services

When the new convert testifies, the people of the church are afforded the opportunity of hearing and seeing him, so that they can meet him personally at the conclusion of the service. A testimony time at the close of the altar service also affords the Christian people opportunity to praise God for answered prayer. Such public testimonies will often lift the sagging spirits of those who may not have seen their prayers answered. You should take your newly saved friend and introduce him to the Christians of the church. In this way each established Christian can offer words of encouragement to the young convert which will mean much to him in the early hours and days of his Christian life. After the new convert has testified and been introduced, the pastor can have the church people lift their hands indicating they will pray for the new convert that night and during the next few days. All of this means much to the new child of God.

—Orville W. Jenkins

67. Victorious Close for Revivals

As the evangelist emphasizes the need to seek God now, he can also remind the people that greater days of soul winning are ahead for the church. On the closing night, after the altar service, it might be profitable for the new converts to be gathered around the altar. The church members could also come, forming a wall of faith, prayer, and friendship around the new ones. The evangelist could speak to the Christians of the responsibility that is now theirs in helping the new converts. He should tell them of the challenge in going forward with the renewed strength that has been gained in the campaign. He could speak encouragement and advice to the new Christians. The pastor should lead the entire group in prayer. This or some similar type of closing leaves the church looking ahead and expecting greater things. A real revival gives the church an enlarged vision.

—V. H. Lewis

3

Visitation and Personal Evangelism

Sometimes debate and even distrust arise between persons who believe exclusively in either personal or public evangelism. The simple facts of how persons come to Christ show that both are desperately needed in every age in every place. Few people ever come to Christ without a personal, individualized ministry to them by a caring Christian who carries a soul burden for them. But it is also true that few people come to Christ without hearing the gospel preached; through the preaching of the powerful Word of God persons come to believe.

So let the friendly discussion between the merits of personal and public evangelism continue. But in our work of ministry for Christ, let us use both; they belong together. Every church needs both, and every Christian is enriched by participating in the full work of both personal and public evangelism. Personal evangelism ideas follow:

68. Power of Personal Testimony

As an aid to making personal evangelism a way of life, I suggest that you develop a concise statement of your personal religious experience—your testimony. Plan it carefully and prayerfully so you can give it in two minutes—whether to a group or to one person.
Major on what Christ is doing for you now as you walk with Him in the way.
Barely touch on the past.
Lift up Christ.
Do not deal in argumentative points of doctrine or belief. Don't talk about what one must give up to be a Christian.
Make your testimony
. . . brief
. . . Christ-centered
. . . positive
. . . radiant
. . . happy
Then it will say to others, "Christ can change your life; He can do all this for you too—and more!"
—Ponder W. Gilliland

69. The Need for Personal Witness in Visitation

The reason some visitation programs fail is that the calls made were only invitations to Sunday School and church.

Those who call must be witnesses for Christ. The appeal of Christ is a greater appeal than a church invitation. Let us all strive to lift our visitation program to the level of soul-winning efforts. People should be invited to our services, but even the invitation is strengthened by witnessing for Christ. He is the great attraction. An invitation to a church service places the call on a competitive level with other churches in the community. Concern over a person's spiritual need lifts the contact to the high level of the greatest appeal—Christ!

—V. H. Lewis

70. Identification with New Convert

To win someone to Christ you must identify with him. To identify with him means to relate yourself to him in such a way as to gain his confidence. This is normally the result of showing an interest in him as a person. Jesus demonstrated this kind of identification in His contact with such people as the woman of Samaria and with Zacchaeus (John 4:7; Luke 19).

—Bennett Dudney

71. Prospect List

Every Christian needs his personal prospect list, for our evangelistic intention must be specific. But we must also be alert for the sudden opportunity, the chance conversation which may start the great thing to happening. Every occupation has its special possibilities. One can think of those unique opportunities offered to homemakers, lawyers, teachers, nurses, doctors, members of labor unions, welfare workers, students. Every social or neighborhood contact offers possibilities.

After the death of a Chicago physician it was said that among the possessions he left there was none so precious to his friends as the little black notebook which contained the list of names of people he was praying for and seeking to win to Christ. It was a varied list, members of his own family circle, doctors, nurses, patients, druggists, businessmen, students, clerks, taxicab drivers, boys and girls of the neighborhood. They were all there—a grand company, all of whom he believed had been committed unto him, and for whom he had a definite responsibility before God. Great was his joy when he was able to note beside the name that that one had given his or her heart to Christ.

A church can produce that sort of members by giving them a great desire to see others won and giving them a start through a lay evangelistic training program. It can urge upon its members the necessity of praying for those whom they would like to see brought to Christ. "If you speak to God about your friends, you will soon find that you are speaking to your friends about God."

—George E. Sweazey

72. Planned Contact for Personal Evangelism

The planned contact may take weeks, months, or even years. Your first task will be to establish confidence in your Christian testimony in the mind of the one you seek to reach. This is done through the life you live, your actions that bear out your concern, and the words you speak. If you are consciously working at trying to establish a beachhead from which you can move into a presentation of Christ, that opportunity will come. Watch for the strategic time! The climax of the planned contact is going to the home or to the person with the intention of presenting Christ and trying to get the person to accept Him.

—Bennett Dudney

73. Casual Contact for Personal Evangelism

Whenever personal faith is alive, evangelism becomes an informal, normal, happy part of daily life. Those who have gotten started in personal evangelism through being given training and assignments in visitation programs often make the winning of others a continual private enterprise. They take seriously the saying, "The supreme business of every Christian is the bringing of others to Christ." A basic rule for all evangelism is this: WHATEVER IS TO BE DONE ALL THE TIME HAS TO BE LEARNED AT SPECIAL TIMES. All of the skills learned in evangelistic visiting are important in this privately undertaken evangelism.

The most striking stories of "personal evangelism" often are of contacts between strangers—in trains or restaurants. People who know they will not see each other again have the fewest restraints. This should not mislead us into making this the typical example. Valuable though it is, it is the least important sort of evangelistic conversation. There is no way to carry it on to a lasting result. We can hope that God will see that what is started will be finished, but His normal way is to have us keep people in our prayers and care until we see them brought into the Christian fellowship.

—George E. Sweazey

The casual contact can be, for example, with the person beside you on the plane, the salesman at your door, or a chance business acquaintance. Although unplanned, the casual contacts are important. Many times they are surprisingly rewarding. You will always find that the Holy Spirit is preparing the person for your witness. This is the reason for the prompting of the Holy Spirit to share your witness. He delights in sending across your path people with spiritual needs. As you develop an alertness to the promptings of the Holy Spirit you will be thrilled at the opportunities that are yours.

—Bennett Dudney

74. Occupational Witnessing Groups

While this group may not seem to be so adaptable to every church, by the very nature of the calling that is used it is often effective. In order to provide prospects for this evangelistic force, a church needs to make a note of the job or profession of church visitors and of the new people contacted by visitation evangelism. This specialized method of soul winning is to have members of like profession from the church endeavor to win the prospect. People in the same line of work have more in common. It is more likely that a doctor could win another doctor to Christ. It would, on the other hand, be more difficult for a person who works in an office to win a mechanic. This special group has been effectively used in a number of churches.

—V. H. Lewis

75. Adult Sunday School Classes Witness

Members of young people's and adult classes should share in the work of personal soul winning. Wise teachers will seek to encourage and guide these activities.

One eighteen-year-old young lady did personal work among the other young women of her town. She would talk with them in stores, on streets, or in their homes. As she talked in her quiet ways girls would weep under conviction for sin. Radiantly happy, she testified humbly that God had helped her to win in a revival the last one of eighty persons on her prayer list.

It requires more skill and broader preparation for a leader to inspire, enlist, and guide the activities of others than it does to monopolize the activities himself. When a leader knows how to engage the entire membership of the class in worthwhile effort, the class members are ready to cooperate eagerly by accepting responsibility; an effective class is the result.

—Mary E. Latham

76. New Converts Witnessing Group

The Andrew's Band is for those who have very recently found Christ. It is based upon the scripture from which it gets its name. In the first chapter of St. John's Gospel, in the fortieth and forty-first verses, we read of Andrew finding Christ and that his first act was to win someone else.

There is no group more eager to work for Christ than new Christians. Even though they may be inexperienced, their sincerity and enthusiasm are in their favor. With instruction and encouragement these new Christians can do much to advance the kingdom of God, but unless there is an organized group for them they will not usually accomplish much in soul winning.

Through the "Andrew's Band" they can be put to work making assigned visits. They can be encouraged to witness to their new-found joy and peace. This activity in soul winning will strengthen them. In this effort for Christ the new converts are blessed in their new, Christian way of life. It is easier for them to make the rather abrupt change between the old, sinful life and the new, Christian pattern. Thus the Andrew's Band is beneficial in two ways. It wins souls for Christ and strengthens those who have recently found Him.

—V. H. Lewis

77. Witness Outline for Children

Really Living outlines the steps of salvation in words children can understand. Here is a brief summary:

1. God loves you and wants you to really live (John 3:16; John 10:10).

2. Oops!
   You can't—because of sin (sin is disobeying God).
   For all have sinned, and come short of the glory of God (Rom. 3:23).
   Say! That means you.

3. What can you do about it?
   Not a thing . . . by yourself.
   For by grace are ye saved through faith; and that not of yourselves: it is the gift of God: not of works, lest any man should boast (Eph. 2:8-9).
   Don't give up . . .

4. Jesus died for our sins (Rom. 5:8).

5. He offers the real life (Rom. 6:23; 2 Cor. 5:17).

6. So, if you really want to live . . . you must repent.
   What's that?
       a. Admit you have sinned.
       b. Feel sorry for your sins.
       c. Be willing to quit sinning.
       d. Ask God to forgive you (1 John 1:9).
   Receive Jesus as your Saviour (Rev. 3:20).

7. NOW
   . . . It's your turn.
   Pray in your own words or make these words your own . . .
   Dear Jesus:
       I admit I have sinned and I am sorry for what I have done. Please forgive me.
       I believe You died for me. I now accept You as my own Saviour.
       Help me to obey You every day. Thank You for forgiving me and making me Your child.
       Amen.

Now you can start really living—
   - Read your Bible.
   - Ask God to help you each day.
   - Let your new life show at home.
   - Go to Sunday School and church.
   - Tell someone else about
     REALLY LIVING.

                  —as quoted by Wesley Tracy

78. Newly Married Witnessing Group

This type of contact is a very pleasant one. It takes advantage of a usually favorable situation. The group consists of two or three newly married couples. Their assignment is to call on those who are just married. The prospects are obtained from the information in the local newspaper or from assistance of the members of the church. To utilize this group to the fullest extent they should call on every newly married couple whose address they can find. This should be done regardless of what minister performed the ceremony, for very often a minister is chosen for convenience rather than denominational affiliation. The call is most effective as soon as possible after their marriage, preferably a day or two after the new couple return from their wedding trip.

—V. H. Lewis

79. Scriptures to Use in Witnessing

Need of Salvation: Rom. 3:23; Isa. 53:6
Result of Sin: Rom 6:23; John 3:18; Ps. 9:17
You Can Be Saved: John 3:16; Rom. 6:23; 10:13; Isa. 1:18; Col. 1:13-14
How to Be Saved:
    Repentance—Luke 13:3; Isa. 55:7
    Confession—1 John 1:9; Prov. 28:13
    Acceptance—Rev. 3:20
    Faith—Rom. 10:9-10; Acts 16:31; John 11:25
    Assurance—Rom. 8:16; John 5:24; Hos. 14:4

—Wesley Tracy

80. Crises Witnessing Group

This group is a small one. Two or three couples can care for it in any church. Their special assignment is to contact anyone in the town, community, or parish area who has any kind of accident. It does not matter if the prospects belong to another church. This program is interesting and will make the church some real friends and give favorable publicity as well as win souls to Christ. All the church members must cooperate and notify the pastor's office or the chairman of the squad as soon as they learn of any accident. Any sort of a calamity that befalls an individual or family can have the attention of this special group.

—V. H. Lewis

81. Friendship as Basis for Personal Evangelism

This is a reversal of some of our "invite them to church" visitation programs, although they are important. Instead of going to their homes with an invitation to church, our first concern is to establish a friendship link with the home. The pattern may be illustrated by the following diagram:

To establish this kind of beachhead in the world will mean the denial of the myth, "Isolation is an aid to holiness and helps the person to live the Christian life." While we have not openly accepted this idea, we often practice it. It is quite normal and proper for us to enjoy the fellowship of

Christians more than that of sinners. However, we should closely examine our motive.

This establishment of fellowship provides a strong foundation for witnessing. It says you are more interested in Jim than in what he can do for you or the church.

—Bennett Dudney

Gospel Presentation Outlines

82. Nazarenes in Action Plan

Here is a useful plan for presenting the gospel. This is an adaption of the Evangelism Explosion method.

INTRODUCTION

1. Their secular life
2. Their church background
3. Our church
4. Testimony—personal and church
5. Questions:
   a. "Have you come to the place in your spiritual life where you know for certain that if you were to die tonight you would go to heaven?"
      Transitional Statement: "May I share with you how I came to know for certain that I was going to heaven (and how you can know too)?"
   b. "Suppose you were to die tonight and stand before God and He were to say to you, 'Why should I let you into my heaven?'—what would you say?"

The Gospel

1. Grace
   a. Heaven is a free gift (Rom. 6:23*b*)
   b. It is not earned or deserved (Eph. 2:8-9)
2. Man
   a. Man is a sinner (Rom. 3:23)
   b. He cannot save himself (Eph. 2:8-9)
3. God
   a. Is merciful; He does not want to punish us (2 Pet. 3:9)
   b. Is just; therefore must punish sin (Rom. 6:23*a*; Exod. 34:6-7)
4. Christ
   a. Who He is—the infinite God-man (John 1:1, 14)
   b. What He did—He paid for our sins and is alive to show us that He purchased a place in heaven for us which He offers as a free gift which may be received by faith (Isa. 53:6)
5. Faith
   a. What it is not—mere intellectual assent or temporal faith (Jas. 2:19)
   b. What it is—trusting Jesus alone for your salvation (Eph. 2:8-9)

The Commitment

1. The Qualifying Question
   a. "Does this make sense to you?"
   b. Acknowledge Christ's presence (Matt. 18:20)
2. The Commitment Question (Invitation)
   a. "Would you like to receive this gift of eternal life now?"
3. Clarification and Commitment
   a. Trust Christ alone
   b. Repentance and confession—"Godly sorrow worketh repentance" (2 Cor. 7:10)
   c. Receive Christ as Savior and out of gratitude make Him Lord

4. Prayer of Commitment (one prayer, three parts)
   a. Pray for the prospect
   b. Pray with the prospect
   c. Prayer of thanks
5. Assurance
   a. "I would like for you to see what Jesus said about what you have done." John 6:47: "He that believeth on me hath everlasting life."
   b. Questions:
   "If you should die tonight in your sleep, where would you go?"
   "If God should ask you, 'Why should I let you into my heaven?' what would you say?"
   "Welcome into God's family!"

IMMEDIATE FOLLOW-UP

1. Spiritual Birth Certificate
2. Commitment to Local Fellowship
3. Basic Bible Study No. 1
4. Commitment to Witness
5. Resist Satan

83. Roman Road of Salvation Outline

(There are several variations. This is one.)

All have sinned	Rom. 3:23
	5:12
Penalty for sin	Rom. 6:23
Payment	Rom. 3:24
Confession & Belief	Rom. 5:8
	10:8-9
	10:13
	6:23b

84. Four Spiritual Laws

Just as there are physical laws that govern the physical universe, so are there spiritual laws that govern your relationship with God.

LAW ONE: God loves you and offers a wonderful *plan* for your life.

God's Love

"For God so loved the world, that He gave His only begotten Son, that whoever believes in Him should not perish, but have eternal life" (John 3:16, NASB).

God's Plan

(Christ speaking) "I came that they might have life, and might have it abundantly" (that it might be full and meaningful) (John 10:10, NASB).

Why is it that most people are not experiencing the abundant life? Because . . .

LAW TWO: Man is *sinful* and *separated* from God. Therefore, he cannot know and experience God's love and plan for his life.

Man Is Sinful

"For all have sinned and fall short of the glory of God" (Rom. 3:23, NASB).

Man was created to have fellowship with God; but, because of his stubborn self-will, he chose to go his own independent way and fellowship with God was broken. This self-will, characterized by an attitude of active rebellion or passive indifference, is evidence of what the Bible calls sin.

Man Is Separated

"For the wages of sin is death" (spiritual separation from God) (Rom. 6:23, NASB).

The third law explains the only way to bridge this gulf . . .

LAW THREE: Jesus Christ is God's *only* provision for man's sin. Through Him you can know and experience God's love and plan for your life.

He Died in Our Place

"But God demonstrates His own love toward us, in that while we were yet sinners, Christ died for us" (Rom. 5:8, NASB).

He Rose from the Dead

"Christ died for our sins . . . He was buried . . . He was raised on the third day, according to the Scriptures, . . . He appeared to Cephas, then to the twelve. After that He appeared to more than five hundred . . ." (1 Cor. 15:3-6, NASB).

He Is the Only Way to God

"Jesus said to him, 'I am the way, and the truth, and the life; no one comes to the Father, but through Me'" (John 14:6, NASB).

It is not enough just to know these three laws . . .

LAW FOUR: We must individually *receive* Jesus Christ as Savior and Lord; then we can know and experience God's love and plan for our lives.

We Must Receive Christ

"But as many as received Him, to them He gave the right to become children of God, even to those who believe in His name" (John 1:12, NASB).

We Receive Christ Through Faith

"For by grace you have been saved through faith; and that not of yourselves, it is the gift of God; not as a result of works, that no one should boast" (Eph. 2:8-9, NASB).

When We Receive Christ, We Experience a New Birth
(Read John 3:1-8.)
We Receive Christ by Personal Invitation
(Christ is speaking): "Behold, I stand at the door and knock; if anyone hears My voice and opens the door, I will come in to him" (Rev. 3:20, NASB).
Receiving Christ involves turning to God from self (repentance) and trusting Christ to come into our lives to forgive our sins and to make us the kind of people He wants us to be. Just to agree intellectually that Jesus Christ is the Son of God and that He died on the Cross for our sins is not enough. Nor is it enough to have an emotional experience. We receive Jesus Christ by faith, as an act of the will.

85. Life Can Have True Meaning

Here are the five steps in this useful soul winning handout.

STEP 1: GOD LOVES YOU and Has a Plan for Your Life.
• His Love Includes You
"For God so loved the world that he gave his one and only Son, that whoever believes in him shall not perish but have eternal life." (John 3:16, NIV)
• He Has New Life for You
"I have come that they may have life, and have it to the full." (John 10:10, NIV)

STEP 2: SIN SEPARATES YOU from GOD and from OTHERS.
SIN is man's walking his own way in rebellion against God's will. When we walk away from God, we walk away from life.
• Everyone Has Sinned
"For all have sinned and fall short of the glory of God." (Rom. 3:23, NIV)

65

- Sin Brings Death

    "For the wages of sin is death . . ."   (Rom. 6:23, NIV)
As sinners we futilely try to find life's true meaning in the ways and places

- Our Own Efforts Cannot Save Us

    "For it is by grace you have been saved, through faith— and this not from yourselves, it is the gift of God—not by works, so that no one can boast." (Eph. 2:8-9, NIV)

STEP 3: JESUS CHRIST DIED and ROSE AGAIN for our sins.

- He Died in Our Place

    "But God demonstrates his own love for us in this: While we were still sinners, Christ died for us."

    (Rom. 5:8, NIV)

- Jesus Christ Is the Way to New Life

    "Therefore, if anyone is in Christ, he is a new creation; the old has gone, the new has come!"

    (2 Cor. 5:17, NIV)

- He Gives Inner Peace

    "We have peace with God through our Lord Jesus Christ."   (Rom. 5:1, NIV)

- And Freedom

    "So if the Son sets you free, you will be free indeed."

    (John 8:36, NIV)

- And Eternal Life

    ". . . but the gift of God is eternal life in Christ Jesus our Lord."   (Rom. 6:23, NIV)

STEP 4: YOU MUST REPENT and ASK GOD FOR FORGIVENESS.

- Admit and Confess Your Sins to God

    "He who conceals his sins does not prosper, but whoever confesses and renounces them finds mercy."

    (Prov. 28:13, NIV)

- Repentance Means:
  - to acknowledge your sins
  - to be sorry for your sins
  - to confess your sins
  - to be willing to forsake your sins
  - to have your life changed by Christ

- Forgiveness Is Promised
  "If we confess our sins, he is faithful and just and will forgive us our sins and purify us from all unrighteousness."   (1 John 1:9, NIV)

STEP 5: PLACE YOUR TRUST IN CHRIST and RECEIVE HIM AS YOUR SAVIOR.

- Christ Is Ready
  "Here I am! I stand at the door and knock. If anyone hears my voice and opens the door, I will go in . . ."
                                                       (Rev. 3:20, NIV)

- Receive Him Now
  "Yet to all who received him, to those who believed in his name, he gave the right to become children of God."
                                                       (John 1:12, NIV)

- What to Pray:
  Lord Jesus, I want to have life. I know that I have sinned. I need Your forgiveness and pardon. I believe that You died and rose again for my sins. I now accept You as my personal Savior. I will forsake my sinful life. I know that Your grace and power will enable me to live for You. Thank You, Jesus, for saving me and for giving me a new life.

A handbook which explains this plan more fully, *Discipleship: Your New Life in Christ,* is available. Quality copies of this plan are available through the Nazarene Publishing House.

86. Personal Evangelism Follow-up

The first four steps in follow-up are:

• Sharing an *assurance verse,* such as John 6:47, with the new convert.

• Presenting a *spiritual birth certificate* to the convert.

• Obtaining his promise to go to church and make *public testimony* of his newfound relationship with Christ.

• Obtaining his agreement to begin a *Bible study,* such as *Basic Bible Studies.*

—Charles Shaver

87. Basic Bible Studies

When one is a new Christian, he is usually very teachable. He must have direction in the Word of God that will not lead him astray. One new Christian said she was so hungry for spiritual truth that she would have looked to anyone who talked of God. While we are trying to lead the new Christian over certain biblical truth on a topic-by-topic basis, he is also being asked to read portions of John's Gospel. The hope here is that a pattern of systematically reading through entire books of the Bible be developed.

One of the goals of *Basic Bible Studies* is to build a habit of life that includes daily Bible study. Wendy, a new Christian having done *Basic Bible Studies,* said the program made her start reading the Bible regularly. Probably this is a result of having a specific Bible study to do and the discipline of having it done by a specific time to meet her appointment with her follow-up worker.

—Charles Shaver

88. Follow-up Resources

The two major weapons of the spiritual adoptive parent are the Word of God and personal testimony. When the convert asks you a question, answer him from the Bible, so you begin to develop the concept that he can find the answers for his problems in the Word of God. As that spiritual child learns the Word, he will find himself able to resist the devil by use of scripture just as Jesus did in the wilderness (Matt. 4:1-11).

Urge the spiritual baby to memorize scripture. There is a memory verse on each study in the *Basic Bible Studies*. He cuts it out, carries it with him in his wallet or pocket, and does memory work. He's hiding the Word of God in his heart so that he won't sin against God (Ps. 119:11). After these verses are memorized, there is a little slot in the colored packet of the *Basic Bible Studies* where they can be stored.

—Charles Shaver

89. Follow-up Advice for Christian Witnesses

Spend part of your time together to renew your acquaintance. Then a rather general and open-ended question about his spiritual life, such as "How have things gone for you spiritually today, Bill?" will help him to be free to share his feelings. Often this is a time of victorious testimony. Sometimes this leads to a sharing of problems you need to hear. To introduce the review of the convert's Bible study, you could say, with an expectant enthusiasm, "Bill, did the Bible study help you?" Regardless of what his response might be, you could say, "Well, let's look at it together."

You will skim through his answers quickly, pausing to talk about every third or fourth answer, if they seem correct.

If he has missed the main meaning of a question, you might say something like this: "Bill, that's an interesting answer you have here, but there's another main thought behind this verse. Let's look it up together." Use the translation he used. Talk about it together. Ask him to quote his memory verse to you. Your total length of time needed for a call is 20 to 60 minutes. Often these follow-up sessions are times of such spiritual blessing and warm friendship that they may be longer.

—Charles Shaver

90. Follow-up Activities

Your work in conservation begins the moment the prospect becomes converted. You should not leave until you have arranged for another visit, given guidance for personal devotions, and left a helpful booklet.

You must accept this responsibility as your assignment from God. Try the following:

- Bring him to church with you and encourage him to give public expression to his faith in Christ.
- Explain the order of services in your church. Let him know what to expect and the reasons for doing things the way you do in church.
- Introduce him to other Christians near his age.
- Explain to him the various phases of the program of the local church.
- Introduce the new Christian to your pastor.
- Invite him and his family to your home. Invite other friends. Help him find new friends to replace those that will be lost as a result of his being converted.
- Be sure he has a Bible.

• Give some guidance in reading the Bible (what portions to begin with, etc.).

• Call regularly—every few days during the first few months. Give him a chance to tell you how he is getting along. If he falls, help him to be restored in grace. Patient, tactful, and prayerful guidance can help establish the person as a Christian.

• Encourage him to witness to others about his new experience.

• If possible take him with you as you make a call on another prospect.

• Talk to him about the importance of church membership and encourage him to enroll in the next church membership class.

—Bennett Dudney

91. Twelve Ways to Help New Converts

1. Make it a point to shake hands and tell them you have confidence in them. Nothing inspires confidence like knowing someone believes in you.

2. Call them occasionally on the phone, share words of encouragement, tell them you are interested in their progress and that you are praying for them.

3. Remember their coming to Christ has meant the breaking of old associations and stepping out alone. Therefore, be a friend and a companion to them. Do this at least until they have had a chance to make new Christian friends.

4. Have them out for a meal, in your home or at some restaurant.

a. Talk about Jesus; show what they may become if they will let Him have His way with them.

b. Do not let the fact that you may be several years their

senior hinder you in this work. Nothing so thrills or inspires a youth as having some older person take an active, personal interest in his living for God.

5. A Christian worker met a young convert on a downtown street just a few days after the latter had been converted. This older Christian gripped the young convert's hand, asked him how he was getting along, pulled him over against the building, bowed his head and whispered a prayer for him, and hurried on. But, oh, what an uplift that experience was to the young man!

6. Take them aside at the church and ask them how they are getting along, pray a short prayer with them, and where possible have them pray.

7. Ask them occasionally if they have any particular matter about which they would like to have you join them in prayer. This will make them feel that you look on them as real Christians and it will both inspire and encourage them.

8. Suggest a promise to them. Quote it, show it to them in your Bible, or write it out for them. Some two weeks after a young man's conversion a man asked him one night how he was getting along. The reply was, "I am having an awful fight." He was advised to go home and read Jude 24, which he did, and on that wonderful promise, "Now unto him that is able to keep you from falling," he won one of the greatest victories of his life.

9. Impress upon converts the necessity of reading the Bible. Urge them to memorize verses and whole chapters, and teach them that it is only as we study and know the Book that we can fully know the wonders of the Christ it portrays.

10. Emphasize the importance of reading good devotional books and magazines. If possible place copies of suitable books and papers in their hands, so they may become familiar with the proper kind of Christian literature.

11. Show them the value of uniting with the church. Church membership is planned by God and every Christian

should have a church home. While the church membership will not save, it will help them to stand.

12. Urge the necessity of being filled with the Spirit. Explain how the Holy Spirit comes to cleanse the heart from carnal self and inbred sin and to fill with divine power for living and serving Him acceptably.

—Jarrette Aycock

92. Make Personal Evangelism Specific

Dr. Paul Benjamin says, "The average person comes into contact with 20 to 30 different people a day." Prayerfully ask God to reveal one or two individuals or families to you and then concentrate on these. We tend to make one of two serious errors in this regard. Either we are too general in trying to reach the whole world, and never get specific in naming any particular one, or we choose too many people and get discouraged when we become bogged down with too much responsibility. One discipler commented, "I'm tired of trying to reach the whole world; I'm going to concentrate on the person God lays on my heart."

—Don Gibson

4

Methods
and Processes
of Evangelism

"By all means save some" is the apostle Paul's powerful advice—that instruction is as good today as it was the first time he said it (1 Cor. 9:22). He used a variety of evangelistic methods. Church planting, revival preaching, personal witness, street preaching, university discussions, pastoral proclamations, and gospel songs from a dungeon were all a part of the mosaic of his soul-winning methods. Processes and methods for evangelism are all for the purpose of bringing folks to Christ and helping them become established in their faith. A variety of evangelism techniques follow:

93. Revival Prayer

Chains of prayer, in which intercession is continuous throughout a whole day, have sometimes been effective. All nights of prayer have often produced far-reaching results.

Group praying before and after the services and throughout the day makes a powerful contribution to the success of a revival. These meetings may be held in the church or in the homes of the people. There is one danger in all organized efforts to encourage the people to pray. That is that prayer shall become mechanical rather than spontaneous. To be really effective, prayer must come spontaneously from a burdened heart. It cannot be primed and pumped up, though without a doubt some leadership and some encouragement in persuading people to pray is almost universally necessary.

—G. B. Williamson

Ideas for Revival Prayer Efforts

• Pray for revival in family devotions.

• Plan prerevival prayer meetings through the various organizations of the church.

• Organize prayer committees. One committee could pray for the evangelist. You cannot afford to have him come in on a spiritual "flat." Another committee could pray for the pastor's ministry; another, for the musicians. The work of the visitation teams could be the prayer assignment of another group.

• Make prayer assignments. Specific Christians praying for specific sinners is the goal.

• Consider whole days, or nights, or half-nights of prayer. One a week for the four weeks before the campaign is an acceptable plan.

• Many churches have used the prayer-partner plan successfully.

• Organize cottage prayer meetings.

• Enlist the prayer help of small groups that exist in your church, or organize new small groups to pray for revival.

• Neighborhood prayer meetings can be effective. These

differ from cottage prayer meetings in that only the people in a certain neighborhood attend a specific meeting.

• Include fasting periods in your plans.

• Adopt a prayer promise from the scripture for the revival. Ask the pray-ers to claim victory in revival faith.

• Plan preservice prayer sessions each night of the meeting.

—Wesley Tracy

Organized prayer meetings need to be announced and promoted. Publicize and push them and the people will pray and the power will fall and the people will come. If you don't, it will not, and they won't.

—John Bisagno

94. Home Mission and Church Planting

In the early days of the Church of the Nazarene the major task of evangelism was to move into a center of population and hold a revival that would culminate in the formation of a new church. At this stage home missions were synonymous with evangelism. The locations needing churches were so numerous that most of the time of the authorized evangelists was concentrated in this area of service.

—Mendell Taylor

Every denomination reporting an increase in membership reports an increase in the number of congregations. Every denomination reporting an increase in total number of congregations reports an increase in members. Every denomination reporting a decrease in membership reports a decrease in congregations. Every denomination reporting a decrease in congregations reports a decrease in members.

—Dean R. Hoge and David A. Roozen

95. Evangelism in the Home

To save their children's souls, parents should plan to spend some time with them to play, to read, to pray, to sing, and to work together. No one can do for children what parents fail to do. So important is it that the family be gathered for Bible reading and prayer at least once every day, that it could almost be ventured that a home is not a Christian home without a family altar. The most important work parents have to do is to train their children in the right way and lead them to Christ.

A very large majority of Christians were converted in youth. A still larger majority of church leaders found Christ in their early years. These facts indicate clearly that if our evangelism does not reach the youth, the church will ultimately fail in its mission.

—G. B. Williamson

96. Building Bridges for Evangelism

Friendships take time and effort. There will be the need for repeated contacts over an extended period of time. This prepares the relationship for the invitation to an event that you feel may meet their spiritual needs. You probably will have to sacrifice some of your normal activities in order to make room for this outreach; but if you do, you will find the joy of becoming involved in building the bridge of friendship.

The time you spend with your neighbor or friend is usually structured around some very natural occasion. Here are some ideas:

- A backyard barbecue involving the entire family
- A morning coffee for women
- A coffee break for men in business
- A ball game or other sporting event
- A hunting or fishing trip
- Recreation at the YMCA or athletic club
- Luncheon engagement with new acquaintances
- A relaxed dinner in your home
- Working together on mutual hobbies
- School activities
- Community events
- An invitation to community church event
- An invitation to your church with a snack afterward in your home or at a restaurant
- A public evangelism event in your church, like a revival meeting.

—Don Gibson

97. Revival Preparation for the Pastor

I have never seen an in-depth revival in any church I served as pastor until first something happened to me. It has been only after revival has become very deep and personal in my own experience that I have seen it happen in the church.

To complete my testimony, I must say more. There have been times when although I have experienced deep and enriching revival in my own life, for some reason it did not spread out and occur in the church. But I have never seen it in the church unless it first happened to me.

—Ponder W. Gilliland

98. Community Survey

An up-to-date list of prospects is needed at all times by a growing Sunday school. A good way to keep the list current is by a regular survey of the community, perhaps once a year. This should be done even in small communities. It is a common mistake, particularly in smaller towns, to believe that the church is so well known that a house-to-house survey could reveal little new information. In many such communities a number of good prospects have been discovered, greatly to the surprise of the workers.

—E. G. Benson and Kenneth S. Rice

99. Guidance for Soul Winners

A systematic plan is necessary for success in soul winning. Adopt a definite program and endeavor to follow it consistently and persistently. The following suggestions will help you:

• Make a list of those whom you desire to win. Don't put it off; make it now.

• Pray for them by name at least once every day.

• In an inconspicuous way, let them know that their names are on your daily prayer list.

• Tactfully try to get them into the Sunday School, the church services, and the revival.

• Give a copy of this list to your pastor and ask for his advice and help in reaching them.

• Solicit the cooperation of a few tactful friends; give them a copy of your list and ask them to pray; occasionally ask them to meet with you for prayer.

• Use the mails. Send those on your list an interesting gospel tract or story, a scripture post card, or write a brief personal letter telling of your concern and interest.

• When you have succeeded in winning anyone on your list, mark off the name and add another.

—Jarrette Aycock

100. Value of Increased Participation

The continued vitality of any organization will rise or fall with its degree of popular participation. No operation that intends to pervade a community can accomplish its goals without the willing cooperation of many people. By decentralizing responsibility and involving a greater number of laymen in evangelistic action, a church may recapture its vitality and move into a pattern of continuous growth.

—David A. Womack

101. Use of Webs of Influence

Webs of common kinship (both the nuclear and extended family), common friendship (friends and neighbors), and common associates (special interests, work relationships, and recreation) are still the paths most people follow in becoming Christians today.

Research conducted by the Institute of American Church Growth of Pasadena, California, on why people come to Christ and the Church, provides astonishing support on the web process at work today. Over 14,000 lay people have been asked the question: "What or who was responsible for your coming to Christ and your church?" One of the following eight responses was usually given: (1) some said a special need brought them to Christ and the church; (2) some responded they just walked in; (3) others listed the pastor; (4)

some indicated visitation; (5) others mentioned the Sunday School; (6) a few listed evangelistic crusade or television program; (7) others recalled that the church program attracted them; (8) finally, some people responded friend/relative as being the reason they are now in Christ and the church.

What percentage of people came to their new relationship with Christ and their church through each category? Here are the results:

Special need	1-2%
Walk-in	2-3%
Pastor	5-6%
Visitation	1-2%
Sunday School	4-5%
Evangelistic Crusade	½ of 1%
Church Program	2-3%
Friend/Relative	75-90%

Here are eight important reasons why identifying and using natural networks of relationships should be the foundation for the outreach strategy of every church:

• It is the natural way churches grow;

• It is the most cost effective way to reach new people;

• It is the most fruitful way to win new people;

• It provides a constantly enlarging source of new contacts;

• It brings the greatest satisfaction to participating members;

• It results in the most effective assimilation of new members;

• It tends to win entire families;

• It uses existing relationships.

—Win Arn

102. Nongrowth Pressures

There are natural institutional pressures operating in every congregation to cut back on the size, variety, complexity, and scope of the total program in order to reduce it to a point that the members can more easily keep track in their heads of everything that is happening. This is a widespread antichurch growth tendency that can be found in nearly every congregation.

—Dean R. Hoge and David A. Roozen

103. Intentional Evangelism Defined

What does intentional evangelism mean? Is it a weekly calling program, or the employment of a minister of visitation, or a series of witness training meetings? Certainly some effort is better than none. Yet research indicates that in a typical church only 1 to 2 out of every 100 people came to their church as a result of a formal visitation program. Intentionality in outreach means doing something. But it doesn't mean doing just anything. More than just good intentions are required. Effective evangelism requires insight and study as to what are the best and most productive intentional efforts that can be made. Some intentional efforts will be more effective in making disciples than others.

Effective disciple-making combines intentional growth principles with an "evangelistic mix" that fits the local church and its unique situation. Tremendous power results in a local church which intentionally focuses on specific growth goals. When staff, lay leaders, groups, officers, and members determine to reach new people and grow, with God's help nothing will stand in their way.

—Win Arn

104. Four Kinds of Evangelism Growth

• *Internal* growth is the development of qualitative growth within the church, sometimes referred to as *nurture.* This involves doctrinal teaching and formation of ethical and spiritual patterns of life, and is the starting point for all other forms of church growth. Without internal growth, the church cannot be the Church.

• *Expansion* growth is the numerical growth of the local church as new converts are won and incorporated into the church. This involves winning people like yourself from the surrounding unchristian society.

• *Extension* growth refers to the *planting of new churches* in the same society as the original churches.

• *Bridging* growth is characterized by the planting of churches across a cultural barrier. This is typical missionary work, whether home missions among people of a contrasting culture, or world missions abroad. The name refers to "bridging" across cultures.

—Paul R. Orjala

105. Take Five for Friendship Evangelism

I know you cannot legislate who people will go to for fellowship, but why not encourage the congregation to take the first five minutes following the benediction to go to people they do not know or do not know very well. Then after these first five minutes let them drift naturally to those with whom they have an established fellowship. It may develop a whole new set of friendships, which in turn will be a modeling concept for the church in *building bridges of friendship* to an outside world. Pastors or congregational leaders could teach this "Take Five" emphasis at the midweek service, and

then merely have a line in the bulletin, following the benediction, which would simply state, "Take Five!"

—Don Gibson

106. Need for Revival Preparation

We have discovered that, just as doctrines can degenerate into mere platitudes, revivals can degenerate into mechanical tradition. We are rediscovering what we have
known all the time—if genuine revival is to come, we must
seek it on purpose. We must plan and pray. Revival will not
just happen, or come about by the mere scheduling of special
meetings or the calling of an evangelist. Most would agree
that proper preparation is at least 70 percent of the success of
any evangelistic campaign. Let us explore areas in which
planning and preparation are most significant.

—Wesley Tracy

107. Evangelism Conscience

A Great Commission conscience is the conviction among
members that their church has the mandate, opportunity,
and responsibility to communicate the gospel to those who
have yet to believe. In the church with a Great Commission
conscience, a disciple-making mentality permeates every
facet and organization of its Body. The result is a genuine
concern by each member for friends, relatives, and neighbors
outside of Christ. A Great Commission conscience is fostered
and kindled by church leaders who exhibit enthusiasm and
devotion to making disciples and constantly hold the

disciple-making goal up as a priority of the church's reason for being.

—Win Arn

108. Assigned Personal Follow-up

One successful soul-winning pastor assigns each new Christian to a seasoned and mature Christian. Mature, spiritual young couples are assigned to newly converted young couples; older, well-established Christian ladies are assigned to unmarried women, etc. The plan works well, for year after year that church and its energetic pastor are effective soul winners.

—Orville W. Jenkins

109. Careful Follow-up Narrows Losses

The real test of our evangelistic effectiveness must ever be—not how many are born, but how many are still living. Warm hearts and careful follow-up narrow back-door losses.

—Charles Shaver

110. Nine Characteristics of an Incorporated Believer

• An incorporated member identifies with the goals of the church.

• An incorporated member is regular in worship attendance.

• An incorporated member feels a sense of spiritual growth and progress.

- An incorporated member has taken necessary steps of affiliation with the Body.
- An incorporated member has new friends in the church.
- An incorporated member has a task or role appropriate to his/her spiritual gifts.
- An incorporated member is involved in a fellowship group.
- The incorporated member regularly tithes to the church.
- The incorporated member is participating in the Great Commission.

Monitor incorporation results. A key and on-going part of effective incorporation involves monitoring new members' involvement in the church. Systematically observing worship attendance, Sunday School attendance, and involvement in small group meetings provides important clues as to the new member's feeling of satisfaction with his/her church life. Closely monitor the involvement levels of each new member for the first nine months of his/her life in the church. And respond immediately at the first sign of problems.

—Win Arn

111. Men and Methods

Men were Christ's method. It all started by Jesus calling a few men to follow Him. This revealed immediately the direction His evangelistic strategy would take. His concern was not with programs to reach the multitudes but with men whom the multitudes would follow. Remarkable as it may seem, Jesus started to gather these men before He ever organized an evangelistic campaign or even preached a sermon in public. Men were to be His method of winning the world to God. He chose twelve from these groups (Luke 6:13).

Having called His men, Jesus made it a practice to be with them. This was the essence of His training program—just letting His disciples follow Him.

When one stops to think of it, this was an incredibly simple way of doing it. Jesus had no formal schooling, no seminary training, no outlined course of study, no periodic membership classes in which He enrolled His followers. None of these highly organized procedures considered so necessary today entered at all into His ministry. Amazing as it may seem, all Jesus did to teach these men His way was to draw them close to Himself. He was His own school and curriculum.

The people you lead in evangelism need you to be with them in tender association and challenging influence.

—Robert E. Coleman

112. Couples' Club as an Evangelism Door

There are vistas in romantic love which give glimpses into infinity. Having a baby is a miracle by which even the most frivolous are awed. This may be why young married people are among the easiest for the church to win. Young people who have drifted from the church are often ready to come back to it again just after they have married. Those who have never felt any need for the church may turn to it eagerly when their children are small.

The young married couples' club is the greatest evangelistic agency in many churches. The youthful high spirits of the members, combined with a new earnest view on life, often makes them the most ardently energetic in winning others. They are at the age when those whose friendships have been largely with the unmarried are anxious to form friendships with other couples like themselves. A church which does not have a special group for young married couples has not opened the door through which the greatest number might be coming into its fellowship.

—George E. Sweazey

113. Cycle of Victorious Evangelism

> Find Them
> Fetch Them
> Feed Them
> Fasten Them
> Finish Them
> . . . and Send Them Forth!

—Stephen Manley

114. Literature as Evangelism Tool

Today, people want literature. More reading is being done now than ever. Sales of religious books are at an all-time high. The "electronic church" evangelists get overwhelming response (and names for their mailing lists) when they make literature, book, or Bible study offers on TV or radio.

Sure, many people watch television and listen to radio. But then they read the newspaper to find out what really happened and what it means! Someone has said, "When printing dies, its obituary will be published on a *printed* page."

Offer Bible studies, tracts, booklets, and other literature during revivals and regular services. Provide outlines or condensations of your evangelist's messages. Some pastors print an outline of their morning worship messages in the Sunday bulletin, allowing the congregation to follow along and make notes.

—John J. Hancock

115. Evangelistic Home Bible Study

Frame a mental picture of the teacher—arm full of Bibles—standing at the door of a comfortable-looking home. He rings the doorbell and waits to be received. Welcomed in the home, he faces a room full of strange people. They look at the teacher with a mixture of expectancy and apprehension. They come from varied backgrounds but they all represent a common need. Each must be confronted with the Word of God. It will not return void. There will be fruit. There will be joy in the harvest. Here is the first home Bible class.

Here are some important suggestions for the evangelistic home Bible study:

Don't forget the names of your guests. You cannot overestimate the appreciation a man has for his own name. You will want to use a guest book and prepare yourself an enrollment list of class members.

Don't forget that extra time your guest spends after the class may be the time he wants to make his decision for Christ, find an answer to a troublesome question, or share the burdens of his heart. What's an extra hour compared to eternity?

Don't forget that many of the words the church uses are unintelligible to the average person. He will not know what predestination or perfection mean, but he will know the meaning of peace, joy, and forgiveness.

Don't forget that unsaved people frequently feel uncomfortable in the presence of Christians. Never start a class with more than three or four Christians in it. Let the sinners outnumber the Christians and they will not be afraid. Counsel each Christian to exercise caution in his conversation. There will be a time to share faith but not theology. If there is a love for the Lord, let it be shared. If there is peace, joy, and hope—the unsaved guest will desire to hear this witness. The Christians in attendance should not interrupt the teacher, but the unsaved guests are encouraged to inquire at any time. After class there will be time for the Christians to share and witness.

Don't forget that you will not be able to keep everyone coming to your class. This is sad, but true. When God's Word begins "piercing even to the dividing asunder of soul and spirit, and of the joints and marrow, and is a discerner of the thoughts and intents of the heart" (Heb. 4:12), some will leave the class. Some never will return, but others will take their places. Hold on in faith and prayer. "Let us not be weary in well-doing: for in due season we shall reap, if we faint not" (Gal. 6:9).

Additional details can be found in the book *The Evangelical Home Bible Class*, Nazarene Publishing House.

—Ira L. Shanafelt

116. Music Revival

Try evangelism through music. Feature a song evangelist or popular gospel music group. The pastor could serve as evangelist. A singer skilled at involving people can organize and use children, youth, and adult choirs. He could form a revival orchestra with local instrumentalists. Some song evangelists are very effective in combining a warm message with their music. Often gospel groups will attract people who would not ordinarily attend. Well publicized, this type of meeting provides an excellent opportunity to acquaint community people with your church.

—John J. Hancock

117. Altar Worker Enthusiasm

Deliver us from altar workers who instruct seekers in the same drab way they would repeat an algebra equation. Let our voices reveal our inner joy with salvation; and let our faces light up when we talk about Him and what He has done for us, and will do for the sincere seeker. The Psalmist prayed that the Lord would "restore . . . the joy of . . . salvation. Then will I teach transgressors thy ways." The altar worker who glows with his inner joy will find it much easier to help the seeker battle through to victory. Enthusiasm can be developed and it is well worth the try.

—Norman Oke

118. Building Dedication Revival

Have you completed the construction of a new building? On Dedication Sunday, launch a week of special services. Your evangelist can be your dedication speaker. Normally, you will have many visitors and prospects present . . . a good time for evangelism. During the week, emphasize inspiration, evangelism, and commitment to the task of outreach in order that God's house may be filled.

—John J. Hancock

119. Sunday School Evangelism

Outward-focused Sunday schools, in contrast to inward-focused Sunday schools, see evangelism and education as two sides to the same coin; two tasks to achieve one goal. Carrying out Christ's commission—to reach and disciple lost people—is the motivation for Christian education in most growing Sunday schools.

—Win Arn and Donald McGavran

120. Sunday School Revival

Reach your largest in-church mission field with a Sunday School revival. Have "Sunday School" each night. Teachers can contact members and visit absentees and prospects. Run the buses and bring in the parents. Classes could meet for a few minutes prior to each service for fellowship or an introduction to the subject of the evangelist's evening message. The evangelist and pastor could meet with the classes briefly from night to night. Consider securing special children's workers to evangelize youngsters while the adult service is in progress.

—John J. Hancock

121. Cradle Roll Evangelism

Babies are wonderful evangelists; therefore, every effort to enlarge the Cradle Roll should be made. Baby-supply stores and photographers watch the birth announcements and send callers who offer to help meet the parents' needs. The Church should be no less alert. Enterprising Cradle Roll management, which works hard at enlarging the roll and at giving the church's help to the parents, can be a mighty evangelistic source.

—George E. Sweazey

122. Adult Sunday School Class Evangelism

An effective program of evangelism can be carried forward in the adult classes in the Sunday School. Leaders and members of such groups are able to invite people of all vocations and of every character. Thus they are brought under the influence of the church and the teaching and preaching of the Word of God. In the lives of many this contact will result in their salvation. Through the avenue of the Sunday School we have an approach to people of the world which is wide open. There are no barriers. The only limits are those fixed by our negligence.

—G. B. Williamson

123. Personal Evangelism with Sunday School Children

Teachers in junior and older departments should find occasion during the year to talk to each unsaved pupil at least once about a personal acceptance of Christ as Saviour or Sanctifier. It is best to find a time when this can be done privately—after others have left the classroom, in the teacher's home after a meal together, on an outdoor hike, across the table in a restaurant, or in the privacy of the pupil's home. If the pupil seems to respond, prayer can be offered to help him find God now. Those who pray through can be encouraged to give a testimony at the first public service. The pastor should be given the written name and address of a pupil who finds the Lord.

—E. G. Benson and Kenneth S. Rice

124. Evangelism Through Parent-Teacher Meetings

A Parent-Teacher Association is a thousand times more needed for a church school than for a public school. Everyone recognizes why parents need to know one another and to know the teachers in secular schooling; all those reasons are vastly multiplied when the schooling has to do with religious faith and living.

Occasions are needed in which parents come to the church to meet their children's teachers and the pastor. They need to be told exactly what the church is trying to do for their children and what is expected of them. They should know about what goes on in the school and what should be done at home to supplement it. These relationships form bridges for evangelism of both children and parents. The child or teen becomes the common bond between teachers and parents.

—George E. Sweazey

125. Public Evangelism in Sunday School

A simultaneous evangelistic service can be held in each department, where a brief message can be given, followed by an invitation. The regular supervisors or other persons, as the pastor or evangelist, can be used for these services. Let the brief message be a positive appeal to love and serve Christ. If there are only two separate departments, there may be one service for children and another for adults. If there is only one department, the children can be seated at the front and the message directed to them. On the morning chosen for these services the class periods can be shortened or omitted. If they are not held during a revival meeting, a good plan is

to hold them at the conclusion of an evangelistic study unit in
the Sunday School lessons.

—E. G. Benson and Kenneth S. Rice

126. Readiness for Evangelism

"Nursery and kindergarten children *can* be saved—it is
not impossible to God.

"Primaries *may* be saved—they often are.

"Juniors *ought* to be saved—the opportunity is ours.

"Teenagers (and older pupils) *must* be saved—the time is
now."

—A. F. Harper

127. Evangelism Committee Useful

In the local church the responsibility for evangelism is
too often left entirely to the pastor. The church board usually
feels responsible to work with the pastor in the selection of
evangelists and the finances of evangelistic campaigns, but
the rest of the work of evangelism is left to the pastor.

A number of churches have successfully overcome this
organizational problem by creating a committee on evangelism. This group usually consists of the auxiliary leaders
and about three others elected by the church. It is vested with
the responsibility of directing and promoting the public and
personal evangelism of the local church.

—V. H. Lewis

128. Pastoral Conference with New Convert

A pastor should have an early personal contact with new
converts either in his office or in their home. He will be able

to ascertain three things: first, he will make sure that the person is clearly converted; second, he will be able to make clear the pastor's relationship to the convert; third, he will be able to tell him about the pastor's class on salvation and church membership.

—C. E. Autry

129. The Variety of Evangelistic Appeals

This is the basic assumption of the Bible: It is normal to be a Christian; it is abnormal to live in sin. Therefore, the following appeals may be used in both public and personal evangelism:

The guilt and consequences of sin
Dread of the future without God
Lost assurance
Boredom with pleasure and possessions
Who am I? and why am I here?
Death
Loneliness
Sense of lack of meaning or purpose
Hunger for truth
Inner civil war
Love of home and family
Magnetism of Christ

—Adapted

130. Invitation Advice

As in all evangelism, the preacher is counting on effects which are far greater than the human causes. He gives the invitation knowing that neither it nor the sermon could be expected to move people unless the Holy Spirit is impelling them. He therefore must do a great deal of praying in advance, and have the sense of praying as he speaks.

The invitation is usually given from the pulpit, though some ministers come down to the main floor level so that they will be closer to the people. An invitation may be woven into the sermon, but it has more effect if it is set apart for its own emphasis. It is better to address it to "Those here who have not . . ." rather than to "Any here who may not have . . ." implying that they are peculiar. The invitation may repeat an appeal from the sermon or the text. It may quote one of the great Bible invitations or promises.

The minister may reinforce the decision with such thoughts as these: The invitation is from God. Christ wants the decision to be made. The decision is a very simple thing, but it will make an amazing difference. The congregation is a loving family, which is eager now to see others come into its fellowship. Continued postponement is a sad mistake. There will be glorious joy once it is settled. The surrender of our lives to Christ has to be definite. He needs us to take an open stand for Him. It will be the most important and the best act of a lifetime.

—George E. Sweazey

131. Mobilize the Whole Congregation

With a group of dedicated people as a nucleus, the church as a whole can be inspired and directed in the evangelistic ministry for Christ. Of course, until this committed minority is present, there is not much use talking about getting the larger congregation involved in the task. Before there can be followers there have to be some leaders. But as the core of trained disciples grows, and the various programs of the church are given more dynamic direction, increasing numbers of people are helped to see their own sphere of ministry.

Total mobilization of the total church for the total ministry is the goal. Actually this is not a role peculiar to Christianity. It is a criterion of success in any enterprise involving people—be it business, government, military strategy, or evangelism.

—Robert E. Coleman

132. Prayer Vigil—Ten Days to Total Obedience and Prayer

Designate a Prayer Vigil Week before the start of the meeting and schedule various types of prayer services. Taking an idea from Pentecost, plan a special emphasis called "Ten Days to the TOP"—*Total Obedience* and *Prayer.* Devote this 10-day period to concentrated prayer by all segments of the congregation, training sessions for lay workers, and intense visitation and "saturation invitation."

—John J. Hancock

133. How to Conduct Revival Prayer Groups

- Someone should be appointed to lead the prayer group.
- Start promptly and end promptly.
    (Allow approximately 30 minutes.)
- Opening of Meeting
    1. Everyone seated and relaxed
    2. Informal—no one standing to lead
    3. Word of greeting and welcome

98

- Scripture Meditation—5 minutes
    1. Short
    2. Conversational style
    3. Read a scripture portion
- Sharing Time—10 minutes
    1. Some blessing from the Bible
    2. An answer to prayer
    3. A witnessing experience
    4. Requests for prayer
- Praying Together—15 minutes
    1. Conversational prayer
    2. Specific prayer
    3. Freedom of participation
- If there are 10 or more people in the group,
    it would be well to divide into several groups
    for the prayer time.
    This will allow everyone to participate
    with less time consumed.

—Manley and Ross

134. Five Revival Prayer Group Methods

Revival Communion

Have a special pre-revival communion service centered around the theme of "Oneness." This is a vital ingredient for revival. The Lord's Supper offers a sacred moment for sharing revival objectives and encouraging commitment on the part of your people.

Prayer Chains

Encourage people to volunteer for this or assign specific individuals to pray during the same time slot each day. Another variation is the "24-hour prayer vigil." Commitments are made by enough people to assure that someone will be praying each of the 24 hours.

Plan an all-night prayer meeting at the church, with persons coming to pray during assigned or volunteer periods. In areas where you have shift workers, this could work very well.

Prayer Cells

Small groups of neighbors or friends can meet together for short prayer periods during the day. This can be done in homes, at work, at school, in car pools, and/or even in the backyard.

Prayer Partners

Two or three people can make a pact to pray together at a certain time each day. A variation is the "Telephone Buddy Plan" . . . two people agree to call each other daily and spend time in prayer together over the telephone. This is a great idea for shut-ins, people in the hospital, housewives, and those working in offices.

Sunday School Class Prayer Meeting

Announce the time and place to the entire class. Send out announcements. This get-together could include refreshments, and the group can meet in a home or at the church.

—John J. Hancock

135. Simultaneous Prayer for Revival

Each week, a specific brief period of time could be announced for the congregation to pause and pray for the revival meeting. An example might be at noon on Wednesday. Insofar as possible, at such a time every person stops other tasks to pray for the revival. Faith will grow as Christians realize that others are praying at the same moment.

—Manley and Ross

136. Guidelines for Altar Workers

Be Ready to Help a Seeker

Step out into the aisle and go to the altar as quickly as possible. The seeker is experiencing both a spiritual and an emotional struggle. Go inside the altar to kneel facing the seeker. Remember, he has come for a meeting with God. Your function is human companionship, human support. You cannot meet his need. You did not call him. So out of these facts grows rule number two.

Spend the First Period of Time in Prayer

As the seeker prays, silently ask God for help for whatever problem the seeker is grappling with. But in these first moments, leave him with God. It may be that you will not be needed in this experience in any function other than this one of human support. You lend your support as the seeker walks to the altar. You lend your support in praying with him so he does not feel alone in front of staring eyes. You are with him, and that is a beautiful gift. It may be the only one needed. But most people, especially those coming for the first time, need human counsel and guidance. So the second function of the altar worker is to offer guidance, scripture, and faith when needed.

Wait Until the Right Moment to Speak

How do you know the right moment? Through verbal cues; when the seeker asks for help. Through nonverbal cues; when the seeker ceases his prayer and looks up to you. When he begins to fidget nervously. When he sighs or his shoulders sag as if accepting defeat.

There are a variety of nonverbal cues that will help you know when the seeker is in need of your help. Be observant as you pray. Be openly sensitive to his spirit. Ask God to give you guidance.

Determine the Nature of the Problem

Never assume that you know the problem and state it. Even if you are right, you may make him uncomfortable to know that his personal problem is so obvious. Ask! And then listen with loving, compassionate, accepting concern.

At this point comes your ministry as spiritual guide. This will require prayerful preparation and knowledge of the scriptures. It would be well for you to mark specific scriptures in your Bible so they are easy for the seeker to see and read for himself when he has need of specific truth. Quoting the scriptures to seekers, especially those who are unfamiliar with the Bible, may be confusing. Let the seeker read what the Bible says. Allow the scriptures to speak directly to him.

Marking your Bible is an excellent way to help in your altar work. You may even want to have notations of scripture on small slips of paper in your Bible so that you can give them to the seeker just prior to leaving the altar. His reading those scriptures on his own is a powerful resource between him and God.

—Bill Vaughn

137. Gear the Church for Conservation

The local church will need to make specific effort to gear itself for the conservation of new converts. This will include developing among the present constituency an understanding of the new convert's point of view. The new convert does not understand all the language of Zion, nor will he immediately live up to all the holiness ethic of a mature saint. Established Christians must be loving and patient about these matters. A Sunday school class for new Christians may be a good idea instead of dropping that three-day-old Christian into a class studying Ezekiel. It's rough on a new convert to get caught in the middle of Ezekiel's wheels.

Besides changing the local church's mind-set, we must develop ways for the local church to show love. Many times Christians have love they would like to share, but the channels for expression of love are not there. Leaders have the responsibility for developing those channels.

—Charles Shaver

138. Altar Follow-up Record

Altar workers can be provided with a card similar to the following:

PRAYER PARTNERS

Pray for one another (Jas. 5:16).

____ Miss
____ Mrs.
____ Mr. _____ Age _____
Address _____

(Where you receive mail)
Home Phone _____
City, State, ZIP Code _____

Bus. Phone _____
What happened to you at the altar:
____ Received Christ as Savior
____ Made full commitment of my life (sanctified)
____ Brought personal problem to God
Name of church you regularly attend _____

Check any of the following that you may desire help with:
_____ Personal Bible study
_____ A Bible study class
_____ An appointment with the pastor
_____ Knowing more about this church
_____ Membership in this church
_____ Special prayer for _____
                Date _____

—Bill Vaughn

139. Guidance for New Converts

Early discipling should include guidance, instruction, and encouragement in these areas:

• Daily Bible reading. Suggest reading the Gospel of John, Psalms, and Proverbs. Start with scriptures which are easy to understand. One of the modern-language versions of the Bible will be most helpful.

• Daily prayer. Suggest 15 minutes a day to start.

• Involvement in church life. Urge the new convert to attend all regular services, enroll in a Sunday School class, become part of a Bible study group, or join the choir.

• Give guidance in how to develop and share a testimony to what God has done in his life.

• Urge the new Christian to be baptized as soon as possible. Pastor, plan an attractive, blessed baptismal service. Give instruction beforehand.

• Get the new convert into a pastor's class. These are planned to prepare the person for church membership. It can be held during the Sunday School hour.

• Encourage family altars. Give literature and guidelines for devotions. Introduce the new convert to *Come Ye Apart*, an excellent devotional quarterly.

• The Sunday School class is made to order to give the new Christian involvement with a small group. It offers Bible study, social events for fellowship, an opportunity for service, and provides personal care by a spiritual teacher. The Sunday School class is still the best established vehicle the church has for small-group ministry.

—John J. Hancock

Endnotes

1. James I. Packer, "What Is Evangelism?" as cited in *Theological Perspectives on Church Growth,* Harvie M. Conn. (the den Fulk Foundation, 1976), 91; James Denney, as cited in *Theological Perspectives on Church Growth.*

2. W. T. Purkiser, *The Message of Evangelism* (Kansas City: Beacon Hill Press of Kansas City, 1963), 16.

3. Minutes of the Sixth General Assembly, 1923.

4. R. V. DeLong, as cited in *Exploring Evangelism* by Mendell Taylor (Kansas City: Nazarene Publishing House, 1964), 624.

5. *Beulah Christian,* 1902.

6. Fletcher C. Spruce, *Revive Us Again* (Kansas City: Beacon Hill Press, 1953), 96.

7. Don Gibson, *Building Bridges of Friendship* (Kansas City: Beacon Hill Press of Kansas City, 1980), 17.

8. G. B. Williamson, *Labor of Love* (Kansas City: Nazarene Publishing House, 1952), 17.

9. Bennett Dudney, *Meet My Saviour* (Kansas City: Beacon Hill Press of Kansas City, 1966), 16.

10. J. B. Chapman, *All Out for Souls* (Kansas City: Beacon Hill Press of Kansas City, 1978 edition), 11.

11. Rosalind Rinker, Source unknown.

12. C. William Fisher, *It's Revival We Need* (Kansas City: Beacon Hill Press of Kansas City, 1966, Revised 1983), 19.

13. V. H. Lewis, *The Church Winning Souls* (Kansas City: Nazarene Publishing House, 1960), 12-13.

14. Mendell Taylor, *Exploring Evangelism* (Kansas City: Nazarene Publishing House, 1964), 26.

15. Purkiser, 35.

16. Ralph W. Quere, *Evangelical Witness* (Minneapolis: Augsburg Publishing House, 1975), 130.

17. Fisher, 66-67.

18. R. A. Torrey, Source unknown.

19. Taylor, 27.

20. Robert E. Coleman, *Evangelism in Perspective* (Harrisburg: Christian Publications, Inc., 1975), 102.

21. Ponder Gilliland, *Winsome Evangelism* (Kansas City: Beacon Hill Press of Kansas City, 1973), 15.

22. Robert E. Coleman, *Dry Bones Can Live Again* (Old Tappan: Fleming H. Revell Co., 1967), 65.

23. Purkiser, 13 (Introduction).

24. Coleman, *Dry Bones*, 15.

25. Stephen Manley and Michael Ross, *Revival Preparation Guidebook* (Kansas City: Beacon Hill Press of Kansas City, 1982), 14.

26. Manley and Ross, 6.

27. Lewis, 11.

28. John J. Hancock, *The Joy of Revival* (Kansas City: Beacon Hill Press of Kansas City, 1980), 11.

29. Wesley Tracy, *New Testament Evangelism Today* (Kansas City: Beacon Hill Press of Kansas City, 1972), 23.

30. Cited in Taylor, 625, 629.

31. C. William Fisher, *Evangelistic Moods, Methods, and Messages* (Kansas City: Beacon Hill Press of Kansas City, 1967), 63.

32. J. N. Barnette, *The Pull of the People* (Nashville: Convention Press, 1956), 7.

33. Coleman, *Dry Bones*, 55.

34. Lewis, 74.

35. Leslie Parrott, *Renewing the Spirit of Revival* (Kansas City: Beacon Hill Press of Kansas City, 1978), 35.

36. Williamson, 48-49.

37. Lewis, 27; Tracy, 99.

38. Spruce, 93.

39. Quere, 17.

40. Ray C. Angell, *Baskets of Silver* (Nashville: Broadman Press, 1955), 95.

41. Williamson, 46.

42. Fisher, *Evangelistic Moods*, 38.

43. Williamson, 75.

44. Hancock, 21.

45. Manley and Ross.

46. Lewis, 34.

47. Manley and Ross, *Revival Preparation Guidebook*, "Program and Altar Workers," 16.

48. Mary E. Latham, *Teacher, You Are an Evangelist* (Kansas City: Beacon Hill Press of Kansas City, 1963), 14.

49. Taylor, 27-28

50. Chuck Millhuff, *The Revival Meeting in the Twentieth Century* (Kansas City: Beacon Hill Press of Kansas City, 1976), 41; Williamson, 74.

51. C. William Fisher, *Evangelistic Moods*, 40.

52. Gilliland, 21.

53. Williamson, 74.

54. Fisher, *Evangelistic Moods* . . . , 36; Williamson, 71.

55. Jarrette Aycock, *Win Them* (Kansas City: Beacon Hill Press, 1933), 9-10.

56. Aycock, 10.

57. Orville W. Jenkins, *The Church Winning—Sunday Nights* (Kansas City: Beacon Hill Press of Kansas City, 1961), 52; and Aycock, 10.

58. Gilliland, 42.

59. Aycock, 26.

60. Parrott, 43.

61. Aycock, 26.

62. Fisher, *Evangelistic Moods,* 42-43.

63. Aycock, 50-52.

64. Fisher, *Evangelistic Moods,* 42.

65. Tracy, 101.

66. Jenkins, 60.

67. Lewis, 30.

68. Gilliland, 109.

69. Lewis, 57.

70. Dudney, 43.

71. George E. Sweazey, *Effective Evangelism: The Greatest Work in the World* (New York: Harper and Row, 1953-76), 133.

72. Dudney, 45.

73. Sweazey, 132; Dudney, 44.

74. Lewis, 84.

75. Latham, 60.

76. Lewis, 82.

77. Tracy, 43.

78. Lewis, 80.

79. Tracy, 36.

80. Lewis, 78.

81. Dudney, 36-37.

82. Don Gibson, *Nazarenes in Action, Personal Evangelism, Manual.*

83. Selected.

84. Selected.

85. Evangelism Ministries, Nazarene World Headquarters (Kansas City: Nazarene Publishing House).

86. Charles Shaver, *Conserve the Converts* (Kansas City: Beacon Hill Press of Kansas City, 1976), 26.

87. Shaver, 51.

88. Shaver, 42-43.

89. Shaver, 46.

90. Dudney, 68-69.

91. Aycock, 67-68.

92. Gibson, 19.

93. Williamson, 75; Tracy, 110; and John R. Bisagno, *The Power of Positive Evangelism* (Nashville: Broadman Press, 1968), 64.

94. Taylor, 627; Dean R. Hoge and David A. Roozen, *Understanding Church Growth and Decline* (New York: The Pilgrim Press, 1979), 351.

95. Williamson, 37.

96. Gibson, 30.

97. Gilliland, 17.

98. Erwin G. Benson and Kenneth Rice, *How to Improve Your Sunday School* (Kansas City: Beacon Hill Press of Kansas City, 1973), 25.

99. Aycock, 42.

100. David A. Womack, *The Pyramid Principle of Church Growth* (Minneapolis: Bethany Fellowship, Inc., 1977), 21.

101. Win Arn and Charles Arn, *The Master's Plan for Making Disciples* (Pasadena: Church Growth Press, 1982), 42, 60.

102. Hoge and Roozen, 347.

103. Win Arn and Charles Arn, 54.

104. Paul R. Orjala, *Get Ready to Grow* (Kansas City: Beacon Hill Press of Kansas City, 1978), 23-24.

105. Gibson, 31.

106. Tracy, 109.

107. Win Arn and Charles Arn, 127.

108. Jenkins, 75.

109. Shaver, 19.

110. Win Arn and Charles Arn, 153f.

111. Coleman, *Master Plan,* 21, 38.

112. Sweazey, 197.

113. Manley, as cited in Hancock, 56.

114. Hancock, 57.

115. Ira L. Shanafelt, *The Evangelical Home Bible Class* (Kansas City: Nazarene Publishing House, 1971), 23.

116. Hancock, 23.

117. Norman Oke as cited in Bill Vaughn, *Training Altar Workers* (Kansas City: Beacon Hill Press of Kansas City, 1979), 24.

118. Hancock, 24.

119. Charles Arn, Donald McGavran, and Win Arn, *Growth—A New Vision for the Sunday School* (Pasadena: Church Growth Press, 1980), 44.

120. Hancock, 22.

121. Sweazey, 191.

122. Williamson, 39.

123. Benson and Rice, 23.

124. Sweazey, 191.

125. Benson and Rice, 24.

126. A. F. Harper, *The Sunday School Teacher* (Kansas City: Beacon Hill Press, 1956), 79.

127. Lewis, 45.

128. C. E. Autry, *Basic Evangelism,* as cited in Jenkins, 77.

129. No source.

130. Sweazey, 175.

131. Coleman, *Dry Bones,* 73.

132. Hancock, 34.

133. Manley and Ross, *Revival Preparation Guidebook,* "Prayer Committee," 15-16.

134. Hancock, 35.

135. Manley and Ross, "Prayer Committee," p. 14.

136. Vaughn, 44-46.

137. Shaver, 39.

138. Vaughn, 54.

139. Hancock, 58.